Flower, Her Buds and a Special Little Blossom

Flower, Her Buds and a Special Little Blossom

A Story of Courage, Faith and Most Especially Love

By Sandy Kamen Wisniewski

Edited by Simone Poteracki

Photography by Janelle Rominski

This book is dedicated to the evolution of humanity and to our beloved animals sharing Earth with us. Our animals consistently remind me how they are our teachers first.

Foreword

I met Sandy in the spring of 2011 when I began fostering animals for Animal Education and Rescue. Over the years, Sandy and I got to know each other. She encouraged me to become a licensed humane investigator, and we went on investigations and rescue missions together. Through Sandy's work as an energy healer, we discovered connections in past lives, perhaps mother and daughter. In 2019, she officiated my wedding.

We learned how well we could work together in other areas as well. Sandy is a writer; I am an editor. In 2016, I edited and published her book *You Are My Sunshine: The Story of a Remarkable Old Dog*. In 2020, we put out *A Dog Named Walter: One Woman's Story of Growth, Searching for a Runaway Dog*. (One fun fact about the Walter book is that the polar vortex of 2019 was the week of my wedding! Sandy managed to juggle searching for an elusive dog in drastically low temperatures and performing the perfect wedding ceremony for my husband and me.)

Like everyone, I have a pandemic story. My experience was mostly positive. In March of 2020, I began working from home. Semi-isolation allowed me to reflect and determine who I wanted to be. It gave me the time and energy to get started on my own journey to physical, mental, and spiritual health and wellness.

One change I made was removing myself from social media.

The sensitive empath in me had always struggled with the negativity plaguing my Facebook feed, and in 2021, I had finally had enough. But being disconnected from social media meant being disconnected from the experiences of others. I learned when reading this book that Sandy's pandemic experiences and perspectives weren't as positive as mine. The closures and restrictions had a negative impact on Sandy and her businesses. However, like many others, the challenges Sandy encountered ultimately led to growth and put her on the path she was meant to be on.

Being disconnected also meant that I had no knowledge of a pregnant dog named Flower, her little buds, nor special Blossom. I was captivated when reading the story, eager to learn more. I was shocked by the impact a dog family could make to those around the world and amazed by the stories of people's struggles and their resolve to overcome them, inspired by a tenacious pint-sized pup with only two legs.

I also learned about the weight the worldwide popularity put on Sandy. Looking through my own negative lens of Facebook, I can't imagine the flurry of emotions she felt each time she opened her window to the world and let everyone in. I know that Sandy has the best intentions and comes from a place of love. I also trust her decades of experience with animals in all situations. I'm sure I couldn't have navigated the overwhelming flood of helicopter followers — well-intentioned supporters creating more difficulty than assistance with incessant "support" and "tips" — and keyboard warriors — those criticizing, attacking, and threatening — as well as she did.

While I'm glad I had no part in the Facebook side of the story, I do wish now that I could go back and be a part of something that touched so many lives. I am thrilled to know the positive impact this adventure, despite its challenges (or perhaps because of them), had on Sandy and her mission in life.

I have witnessed Sandy's evolution over the years. I've seen her open up about struggles she previously kept private and show her true self to the world. (And I believe honesty and vulnerability are two of the most beautiful things a person can display.) I've witnessed her finding her purpose and coming into her role as a healer. And, from one book to the next, I've seen her growth as a writer.

I look forward to witnessing the continued opportunities for growth that upcoming challenges will pose for Sandy and the stories that will unfold because of them.

— Simone Poteracki

Acknowledgements

This book would not be complete without thanking every single person that helped me along this journey to making it complete.

First and foremost I need to thank my soul mate, best friend and partner in every way, Chuck. As I believe I shared in depth in this book, we have a bond that is deep and layered with history and purpose. There is absolutely no doubt that with your participation and heart-centered commitment I have been able to help in ways far larger than I could ever have done myself.

Next, I want to thank Nikki for your ongoing support and dedication to animals, to me and to AEAR as a whole. You are one of the bravest people I know and have a heart of gold. You are my little sister in my soul and heart and I look forward to sharing a full and purpose-driven life with you.

Then there's my sweet friend and dedicated volunteer Julie. Your gentle and sensitive heart is an inspiration. You bring with you every time I see you the compassion that all the animals need that come to us broken. You help ease their suffering and give them the gentle love they need. I trust you completely and the world is a better place because you are in it.

To Lauren, my second daughter-of-the-heart, thank

you for your help in this season of our lives. You were a huge part of this story and all my memories of this incredible time interweave with you in them. I so admire your ability to love with all your heart and your empathy toward animals and humans.

To my editor, Simone, thank you for your dedication to the process of editing this book. I love working with you. Your strength isn't mine and our teamwork to get this done is seamless and leads to a great story. I never take for granted that we have this beautiful partnership. Beyond the work we share you are my soul daughter and a very important person in my life. You give me great hope for the future. Keep learning, growing and finding your courage as we enter this new stage of human growth.

Finally, to everyone else…the volunteers who helped with the puppies, the people who donated money and supplies for their care, those who adopted the pups, those on social media that cheered us on, prayed for us and spread the message of love…thank you. It is together, all of us, that we will make this world a place that will be centered in peace, joy, meaningful connections and love.

In love and gratitude,

Sandy Kamen Wisniewski

Prologue

Gathering in the auditorium within the Akashic Records the Wisest of the Wise watched the screen before them. Mashia, one of the souls who has spent countless lifetimes learning and growing, stood before the blank screen and said to the glowing room of souls, "Earth is going through a very hard time now. It is of great concern and we need to do something to help humans find their way. Please watch."

Mashia lowered her light field and the screen came to life. Before them Earth came into view. Its blue-green color was unmistakable and slowly the scene brought them closer and closer to it. First they saw vast oceans, large landmasses and then slowly the screen moved in closer and began flashing scenes throughout the world – humans in their homes, anguish on their faces, fear vibrating throughout the whole world.

Great sadness swept through the auditorium as the Wise Spirits took in the anguish and suffering, concerns weighing heavy on their souls. They had all experienced lifetimes as humans and they knew what it felt like to feel these dark emotions personally.

The screen went white and images were gone and Mashia moved forward again. "Earth is in crisis. We are asking for a committee of Wise Ones to come together to help with a solution. Which of you has time and feels it in their heart to help?"

Raising their vibrations Wise Ones scattered throughout the room indicated their ability to help and therefore a subcommittee was formed. "Thank you, my friends," Mashia said softly and with love. "We shall convene shortly to discuss further. Thank you to all who attended today. In light and love," Mashia raised her vibration and in response the entire room raised their vibration in love.

Chapter 1

Navigating each decade of my life up until now I always had this undeniable feeling that I wanted to help the world in a "big way" as I always said to people. For decades I thought that this way of feeling was typical of most people, but over time I observed that most people didn't feel that way at all.

But as the years went by it seemed as if each time I came close to becoming well known through the books I wrote, the speeches I gave, the times I was on television or radio, the door shut before I could get my message out globally. I knew that without drawing people in toward me I couldn't share my important message. Without a platform on which to stand I couldn't shout above the masses.

What IS my message? Early on I wasn't even sure what it was, but in the past decade or so it became crystal clear. It's simple really: Love is the answer to everything. When we all learn to live our lives with an open and loving heart, burning from within us and radiating out, we will change the world for the better. That's when we will snuff out darkness and live in a higher vibration of peace, connection and love.

***

I heard, "*Walk — just walk. You will find the answers you seek by moving your body and opening up your heart and mind."* So I did. I began taking these very long walks. It was 2014 and my marriage had been dismal so long that the weight of it was becoming too much for me to bear. I carried with me so many hardships from my past. Life was getting shorter and I needed something big to change…and soon. I began formulating a plan to get out of my marriage of 25 years.

It was a dysfunctional and destructive marriage. We were set in patterns that we created over the years that kept us looping back to those unhealthy behaviors over and over again. My husband Chuck was the angry person, easy to blow up, curse, spit out all his negative feelings and observations about this world and most of the people in it.

I was the enabler, trying to keep the peace at all costs, fighting for the light as I saw it but walking up a mountain of doubt yet stubborn determination. I pushed through life in a constant state of giving to others and sacrificing myself in some sort of psychological state of survival. My drink of choice was being the martyr, the savior for others and the savior of animals. I was righteous in my beliefs to help others but consistently forgot the one person who should have been at the core of my love…me.

We were both very unhappy with each other and our lives as they were at that time. We had finished raising our first two children. Both of them posed challenges for us as they were growing up, but one had extremely serious mental illness since she was about 11 and caused incredible suffering for all of us in the family. We were now raising our grandson Danny, whom we refer to as our son, and life had been very turbulent. I was completely out of steam and my light so dim I either needed to get out of the marriage or be done with this life all together. *This life as I was living it*, I said to myself too many times to count, *was not worth living.* I was utterly spent, exhausted and done.

So I walked and walked...or *went on a journey*, as I would say to myself...searching for myself. It was on those long and cleansing walks that I started feeling this strange and vibrant energy beginning to come off my skin like water vapor radiating off grass on a cool fall morning.

Over time and on those walks the energy grew and expanded around my body. Intuitively I "knew" that if I directed and focused that expanding energy onto people I could help them...maybe even heal them.

At the time I was seeing a gifted therapist named Sharon. One day, during our therapy session, I decided I needed to share with her the strange phenomenon that was happening to me. Either she would say I was officially cracking up or she would help me to understand what was happening to me.

"I've been taking these long walks. As I walk I can feel this energy coming off my skin. It started in my hands, then up my arms, then my shoulders and upper back. After a while of this happening it felt like I could shoot energy out of the palms of my hands and from my fingertips. If I direct my attention on a person I could shoot that energy toward them as if healing them. Is that crazy?"

Sharon looked at me totally unfazed and said, "Not at all. I knew you were a shaman, a healer. I was just waiting for you to figure it out for yourself." I was stunned.

With that, Sharon shared with me her experience with Reiki, an ancient energy practice, and told me to look up Reiki and what a shaman was and go from there. From that day forward I immersed myself in learning through books, classes and certifications. I practiced my healing on friends. My gifts grew over time and practice to include energy healing of the chakras, energy system, the fields around the body and the physical body.

Through energy healing I honed into my sixth sense. My sixth sense, my intuition, tapped into an energy system that allowed me to see and connect with passed souls and wise teachers not currently in human form. Formerly being agnostic and believing there was likely nothing after this life I was baffled, in awe, relieved and thrilled that there was so much more than this life I was living in. In time and practice I would be privileged to communicate with many souls who crossed over and share their wisdom with their loved ones, thus helping the loved ones still on Earth to heal.

If you are new to the concepts I am describing now I hope you will choose to keep reading and have an open heart and open mind. The "old" Sandy would have been incredibly skeptical, BUT I was always open

us on a path together that circles back to this story and this time lining up just perfectly.

Chapter 2

It was the spring of 2021 and my friend Nikki and I were in Michigan at my sister's vacation home. It was a week of rest and relaxation just a few blocks from Lake Michigan in the tourist town of South Haven. It was Saturday night and we were sitting at the dining room table talking.

"Have you ever heard of a woman named Barbara Marx Hubbard?" I asked Nikki.

"No, I haven't."

"She's this world visionary. She's a person that believes that the world will come into their sixth sense through technology. She believes that the best of the best — scientists, teachers, people in medicine, spiritual leaders and more — will come together through the Internet and reach a higher level of compassion, understanding and peace for all of humanity."

Nikki was fairly new to energy healing, metaphysical ideas and to the philosophies of the evolving world from a spiritual standpoint, but she was open to all of it. I met Nikki through the humane society and animal rescue I run called Animal Education and Rescue. She adopted a cat from us six years before and followed us on Facebook ever since.

A year before we became friends I reached out on Facebook looking for a referral to veterinarian that treated rabbits. At the time she worked for an animal hospital in our area and agreed to connect us with her animal hospital. I remember the first time meeting her.

Chuck, Lauren (a young woman I'll be sharing more about later) and I drove to the animal hospital to pick up eye medication for a rabbit in our care. It was the summer of 2020 and the beginning of what I call "the shutdown," when Covid 19 was first announced to everyone around the world.

Fear was mounting in the world about the severity of the illness. The uncertainty and unknown factors surrounding the virus were putting everyone on edge. The government put us on lockdown in the spring of 2020, shutting down schools and restaurants. In our state of Illinois our governor enacted mask mandates and social distancing in public.

As the days stretched on people became more and more fearful of each other. I was fortunate that I worked from home and that Chuck always did the grocery shopping. I wasn't seeing all the new rules playing out in person, so that certainly helped me from not joining the epidemic of fear that was sweeping the world. I wouldn't wear a mask and was avoiding all public places. Self-isolating was truly a blessing in disguise because I was fairly shielded from the fearful energy growing everywhere.

The day when we pulled into the vet's office parking lot Nikki came outside, poked her head in the car and handed us the medicine. I was in the front passenger seat. "Thank you," I said gratefully. "How much do I owe you?"

"Nothing," she answered in a New Zealand lilt.

"I got it."

"You sure?" I asked, surprised and touched.

"Positive, no problem," she said in her sing-song voice. She stepped back and waved goodbye.

Pulling out of the animal hospital's parking lot I said, "That sure was nice of her."

When an experience with another human plants vividly in the memory of the mind it often means that there will be some kind of meaningful and important connection between you and that person. Sometimes you will know exactly what that is in the future and other times you will never know. The clarity in which you "see" the shared connection largely depends on your ability to sense things with your third eye or "sixth sense" and whether the relationship itself is what's important or just that one exchange you had that was important.

With Nikki, that one exchange, for me, planted a seed and I kept thinking about her. By no coincidence I began seeing her posts on social media. Facebook was the only social media platform that I followed regularly, mostly to promote my businesses and to share information about what I was doing. It was the most effective form of communication we had for Animal Education and Rescue. We received more donations through Facebook than any other means.

But it was on my personal Facebook page that I saw Nikki's posts and saw that she was selling soap, trying to raise money as she went through cancer treatment. She needed to have a blood transplant.

"Ask her if she knows what an energy healer is. A

healer can help her," I heard communicated though my intuition. Hearing this message numerous times in a short time I knew the message was real and clear, so I reached out to her on Facebook. Nikki said that she had a friend that was an energy healer and was working with her on occasion, so I thought, *Okay, that's that then.* But then I asked her if she had a GoFundMe page to raise money to help her during and after her cancer treatment. She said she didn't but was thinking of starting one. That was the beginning of our relationship, when I helped her get the GoFundMe page up and running.

After setting up the GoFundMe page I offered to do pro bono energy healing for her since her healer wasn't as readily available as she needed at that time. Through healings and spiritual coaching I learned more about Nikki and assisted her as she navigated a very, very difficult and scary time in her life. I am so thrilled to say that, as of writing this, Nikki is cancer free and happier than she ever has been in her life. She is one incredibly brave woman who has been on a remarkable journey of growth.

Sitting at the dining room table listening to me explain to her who Barbara Marx Hubbard was, Nikki looked at her phone. Typing away and looking back up at me, she said, "Oh, she died."

"Oh, that's so sad," I said. "She was incredible. She had a light that shined from her and was so beautiful. She was an amazing visionary. I believe so strongly in her vision. This time in history, with

"Can you tell what they are wearing?" I asked her. I knew from doing this type of work that seeing what they were wearing would give a clue into the era that we were in.

"I see men wearing some sort of hat, like boulder hat. Everyone is wearing clothes that looks to be like from the 1920s or '30s."

"Do they see you?"

"No, they are walking all around me." She paused, "Okay, wait — the men in the boulder hats are tipping their hats to me."

"Can you try and communicate with one of them?"

(Pause)

"They are smiling, but they don't see me."

I waited a minute letting her just be. Then I said, "What's happening now?"

"Suddenly everything is dark. I am in a forest, I think. It's a little scary."

"Don't worry — I'm with you," I said.

"There's lights all over, like balls of light."

"Can you tell what it is?"

"No, just balls of light…"

"Okay, are there any people?"

She paused and I could hear her sigh deeply. "I see people in shadows walking."

"Can you stop one of them and ask them what's going on?"

I heard her sigh again. "Okay, one of the people said, 'there are Lightworkers scattered all over the world.'"

"Anything else?"

"No." I heard her breath deeply again. We sat in silence for a minute and then she began, "I see people walking toward me. They don't see me and they are walking past me. They look like families or a bunch of people together. They are wearing simple clothes—I can't really tell what. They don't see me."

Prompting her, I said, "Can you sense where they are going?"

"They are moving. They are leaving where they are and going somewhere new."

"Okay, just watch what's going on. I'm going to try and channel Barbara now." I shifted my energy to the portal I had created in my body and waited.

I breathed slowly and dropped my energy deeper. Then I heard and said, "I didn't get to finish what I started." It felt strange and foreign with the words coming out of my mouth. "I'm working on this side to help humanity and Earth, but it's not the same. It's harder since I'm not there. But I'm continuing with the Elders here and doing what I can, but I feel like it's urgent now."

I could see in my mind's eye a rustling of sorts and quick movement but couldn't pinpoint what it was. It was like an expression of what it would be like to have someone rush to a desk filled with papers and shuffle hurriedly through the papers trying to find what they needed.

Putting that energy channel aside I went back to my energy system and said to Nikki, "Okay, Nikki, is there anything else you see or feel?"

"No, nothing."

Shifting back over to the Barbara energy field I opened my throat more and let go completely. I heard my voice say, "You and Nikki are going to help change the world and make it better. You both are part of the group of people who are going to change the world for the better. I don't quite know how yet," I could sense that rustling of papers again, "but you will. And I will be here on this side doing my part."

I could feel Barbara's energy fade away. I took a deep breath and shifted back to my energy system and slowly went through the process of coming out of the trance state. Then I led Nikki out of the deep state.

"Now you can slowly open your eyes," I instructed her. I opened my eyes and met Nikki's eyes and said, "What was that?"

"I don't know. That was weird," she said.

"Yes, it was. I think I really did channel her. I really do, but it doesn't make sense what she said. What could we possibly do to help heal the world now? We aren't famous; we have no way to share any messages with the world."

"I know."

We sat in silence in our own thoughts. "And I wonder who those people you saw were," I said.

"It's like they were all picking up and leaving one life to start a new one. And no matter how I tried to get them to communicate with me they just kept walking around me as if I wasn't there."

Thinking about what she said about the people in the city and the 1920s–1930s attire I remembered,

"Barbara would have been born and lived in that era, with the city and the clothes."

"Oh yeah, I guess that's true."

"And as far as the forest, that goes along with what Barbara said about our future, like shifting from one place to another." I paused.

"Well, we did it," I added. That was fun and interesting, but I have no clue what it means. We'll just have to see."

Chapter 3

In April 2020 we received notice from our 12-year-old son Danny's school that they were closing the school because of a virus. They were concerned about the safety of the children. It was shortly before the school's spring break. I was working from home as usual running both my companies, Animal Education and Rescue, a non-profit animal rescue humane society, and Mindful Spirit, a holistic health and wellness business.

I started Animal Education and Rescue (AEAR) in 2003 shortly after having to put my first dog (as an adult) to sleep. It was in his memory and the childhood animals I had growing up that I was inspired to start AEAR and my work saving animals through the non-profit organization. It was a huge daily commitment that filled my everyday life with both joys and sorrows. In 2008 I wrote a book called *The Animal Warrior,* which chronicled my life with animals. By 2020 I could have written another book just as thick with the endless stories of the animals that have touched my life.

Through my company Mindful Spirit, I do energy healing, spiritual coaching, mediumship, intuitive reading and guided meditation. At that time I had been renting space from a chiropractor's practice and it had been working well for me for many years. After everything shut down I lost my office space. About eight months later, as government restrictions lightened up and people were a bit less fearful I began offering my services in my vintage 1966 *Decamp* trailer that served as an office and meeting space. That ended up being the best thing for my company and for me. It's convenient for me and my clients love the energy and space in my trailer.

When the government shut down the schools and businesses were either closed or were greatly regulated, there was a domino effect. People began working from home, most traveling stopped and restaurants were greatly restricted or closed down temporarily. All of those changes directly affected our other business, The Pet Sitters of America (PSA).

PSA is a pet sitting service I began in 1987. We provide dog walking and overnight care for clients' pets in their homes. With the new changes PSA lost all business because no one was going anywhere. We told Donna, our long-time office assistant, that she could stay home and when things went back to normal she could come back. She was part of our staff...and really part of our family...for 15 years. I still think of her often and feel a sense of sadness that we never really got to have a formal goodbye...at the time we thought it would only be a few weeks.

Since 2008 Chuck ran PSA. Suddenly he was without a job. Almost overnight, in 2020, we lost 75% of our income. Fortunately we have always been frugal and mindful of spending, so our monthly bills were low and we weren't in a dire situation. Thank goodness we've always lived well within our means.

Over the course of the next year fear mounted everywhere around the world. Small businesses closed all over our area and across the US because they couldn't sustain themselves with the government restrictions in place.

In the autumn of 2020 Danny started middle school through the public school but at home remotely. Within a few months we realized what a disaster the remote schooling was for Danny. He was failing all of his classes. We couldn't get ahold of any of his teachers and couldn't even get an appointment with anyone. I had friends who were teachers at that time, so I had a decent idea of what they were going through and I didn't necessarily blame teachers for what was happening.

Our particular school district had not planned ahead for such an event as what was happening, so the administration was scrambling to come up with curriculum. Teachers were trying their best to learn a completely new way of teaching and in my opinion just couldn't handle it.

Many years before I had researched home schooling when my older son was in high school. For different reasons he was struggling in public school, so we pulled him out and he went to the local college for classes. But since that time so much has changed as far as home schooling. I learned of countless topnotch online home school programs for all age groups. There were also different styles of learning.

We found a school that worked on a mastery-based concept where the child had to master each concept before moving onto something else. It had excellent reviews and we could afford it. I decided to pull Danny from public school and have him learn at home. It was the best decision I made for him. It quickly became a bigger blessing because he was learning more than he ever did in public school. There were so many unexpected blessings that were beginning to unfold for us.

***

Depression and anxiety were at an all-time rise all over the country...likely the world. Alcohol and drug abuse increased. Many people were gaining weight and becoming more sedentary. Vast numbers of people felt terribly disconnected from everyone...their extended families, their friends and their neighbors.

Children born and young at that time were completely isolated from the outside world. That creates great challenges for them. They are not exposed to the thousands of opportunities to learn social cues from a wider society than their immediate family unit. The psychological damage would reveal itself later as schools opened up.

Most people were terrified of getting sick. The major media sources were relentless with their reporting of the virus and their take on it. They were brilliant at using words and phrases that were like jolts of electricity, shocking everyone's systems who watched/heard/read the news. If you analyze the emotional charge of the words that were the "new normal," another phrase that was commonplace, it was incredibly damaging.

The words and messages were terrifying and created a great divide with everyone. This, I promise you, is totally counter to the fact that humans need each other and by nature are deeply connected. The covert psychological damage was immense. Fear and anxiety reverberated outward at an alarming rate.

Everyone all over the world was trying to figure out what was happening. I, like many, was on a path to figuring out my perception of it all. I was not filled with fear like most people around me, but there were logical reasons for that.

Keep with me here. There's logic and a reason I am sharing so much of this time in history in this book. It leads us to the big event and the big impact. I promise. I'm not trying to convince you of anything or convert you to my thinking. I'm only giving you my perspective and experiences, which matter to the direction of this story.

It had been years since I watched the news regularly. Frankly, looking back I don't know if I *ever* regularly watched the news. I always felt strongly that the news was a train wreck, sometimes literally but most certainly figuratively. I always felt worse after watching, reading or listening to the news.

For every 10 scary and negative news reports, there may be one positive or neutral story thrown in. I have been empathic (highly sensitive) my whole life.

That means that I can feel things more deeply than most and can absorb negative energy easily.

My healthy way of living was always leaning toward positivity, goodness, kindness, gratitude and love and away from negativity and dark energy. As far as the news went people said things like, "Well how are you going to KNOW what's going on?" I always answered that, "If there's something I really need to know or if there's something that I could do to help, then someone will tell me about it and then I can take action accordingly."

But one of the big changes for me beginning in 2020 was the disconnection I felt from my sisters and my mom. We had very different viewpoints about what was happening regarding the virus, the new rules, etc. Practically and philosophically those differences created a passive and mostly silent wedge between us…at least from my perspective. It was very painful for me for a while. I grieved the loss of my family and our in-person gatherings and our closeness. It frustrated and disappointed me that we didn't see eye-to-eye. But after some time, lots of tears and personal growth I got used to the "new normal."

***

Part of my path, as is the journey of every human on Earth, is to go through difficult emotions. While I may have been protected, to an extent, from the fear sweeping the world I was not protected from my own pain and suffering. Mine came in a way unique to my situation and viewpoint.

During that time there were a few months where I was very angry toward the government for what they were doing and I was angry with the state I lived in for their viewpoint on the virus. I was angry that the government made the choice to shut down businesses and thus shut down our company as an after-effect of their choice. It cut our income down drastically. I was also furious that the businesses that I worked so hard to build, that were essentially my babies, were taken away from me without my input or decision making at all.

The Pet Sitters of America, the company I started at age 19 and nurtured and worked so hard to grow for decades, was gone because of the government...poof. Decades of hard, hard work and dedication to our clients and their pets were gone with a swift shutting down of everything.

Also, I disliked and still don't like facemasks. I feel claustrophobic in them to the point of severe anxiety if I wear one. I literally feel like I can't breathe with one on.

Furthermore masks separate people emotionally and psychologically, since you can't see facial expressions. You can't see people smiling, you can't hear them clearly, you can't read each other and subconsciously that drives a deeper wedge between humans. Being empathic I KNEW all this and the whole use of facemasks frustrated me deeply. A constant state of frustration is not a good state to live in.

Lastly about facemasks, I believed and still do, from doing extensive research, that they are largely ineffective from a health standpoint and they are damaging on many levels. But I was in the minority in that way of thinking (and many ways) in our state of Illinois. I was well aware that I had no control over what other people thought or did. I don't like conflict, so I just stayed home all the time. Other than walks outside I believe I didn't go anywhere public for close to a year. This would turn out to be a blessing because it allowed me to work on myself, my attitude and to be in a good place when the time was right. Good things were coming, really good things. I just didn't know it yet.

Now, some of you reading this will disagree with my viewpoint and that's okay. Whether we agree on how the world got to where it was, who caused it, how it affected us and what needed to be done to deal with it is only relevant to the extent that it put me in a state of mind and spirit to help in a way that I never thought I would...or at least had given up on.

My life-long goals always have been to spread love, joy and peace everywhere I went. I wanted people to understand the importance of living a heart-centered life and to navigate life learning to treat people kindly. I try and remind people that we are all connected and when we connect in love and compassion that we...all of us...are at our best.

In 2020, every day, through small actions and reactions I saw people disconnecting from other people, which was never, ever going to serve humanity's growth. Instead what was happening in the world was going to destroy us if we didn't rise up and shine our light into the darkness.

Chapter 4

As the months in 2020–2021 went by I worked on myself. I found ways to find joy and peace. I took long walks in beautiful soul-filling places in nature. I listened to powerful, positive, uplifting music. Chuck and I grew closer in a new way since our companies had closed or slowed down. We watched movies and discussed books we were reading. Chuck started spending time each week with childhood friends. They had a band of sorts where they jammed weekly. Chuck is one of two drummers.

Of course we tended to the day-to-day tasks of the revolving and ever-needing crew of animals that were in our care. The animals and Animal Education and Rescue became full-time jobs for both of us and having him around more to help me was wonderful. We spent more time talking about how we felt about what was going on in the world and how our lives were changing.

I found a local support group that met twice a month that was growing larger each meeting with people who didn't like what was happening in the world. It was comforting to know we weren't alone in our viewpoint. The group participants gave us a wealth of information and resources based on scientific research studies to back up what we initially perceived. Because most of the people in our lives felt differently than we did it was reassuring to know that we weren't alone and I didn't feel like a crazy person.

With my lifestyle as it was and the fact that I never followed mainstream news and had limited contact with fear-driven people I developed a growing faith in the process of what was happening in our world. I was never afraid of getting sick or dying and wasn't afraid for my family either. Not that I didn't care—I did enormously. I just wasn't afraid in general. There was great power in not living in fear. But frustration and resentment were negative emotions, so I had my own work to do.

As I worked on my growth a powerful, positive outcome unfolded. I claimed a higher state of inner peace. As I always tell my clients, "It is when you crack open with pain and suffering that true growth can begin to take place." Resentment and anger are not healthy to marinate in and in due time I came out stronger on the other end.

***

A consistent life preserver for me is my meditation practice. Almost daily I meditate. I meditate sitting, walking, while doing dishes or folding clothes. Basically any time I focus on my breathing I meditate. One day in the spring of 2020, as I sat on the bed in my trailer, facing my sacred alter space, I felt an intuitive need to pick up a pen and begin drawing. Being a writer was a natural and lifelong passion and part-time income for me, but drawing was never anything I considered one of my strengths. I dismissed any notion of drawing or painting anytime the idea was presented because of my tremor.

I have an inherited neurological condition called Essential Tremor. In me it mostly affects my hands. If you were to observe my hands doing small motor tasks it would look like I had way too much caffeine. Fatigue, lack of sleep, fear, anxiety and lack of food are some of the things that can cause my tremor to be far worse and really handicap me. So I am pretty mindful of taking good care of myself and not getting worked up about things. I limit my caffeine intake and eat regularly.

Essential tremor affects over 10 million people. It took me decades to overcome my social embarrassment and understand and accept my limitations. Through my personal journey I wrote a book called *I Can't Stop Shaking: More Than 10 Million People Suffer with Essential Tremor*. But I would soon find out that I can do much more than I thought I could.

The doodling that started with a notebook and a pen graduated to purchasing drawing paper and colored pencils and finally to plunging into using acrylic paint and canvas. In a short time I became obsessed with painting. The therapy of finding my voice and expressing my feelings through the paintings brought me peace and a sense of strength and clarity. When I painted I was completely present and in the moment. I furiously painted every free moment I had.

Observing what was happening to me, Chuck began painting again after decades since his study of art in school. We began to paint together. My paintings were mostly of animals, people, beaches, moons, lakes and woods. I also painted abstracts and modern-style pieces. Chuck painted landscapes sometimes with barns or buildings. At my urging he dabbled in abstract and fun, whimsical landscapes and buildings. We sometimes did pieces together, him doing the landscape and me adding the animals, people or both.

***

By the fall of 2020 most animal shelters and animal rescue organizations adopted out most or all of their animals. People were scrambling to adopt animals. People were cooped up in their homes and rationally thought it was an opportune time to add a pet to their family because they had the time. Also, some people were scared and depressed and they reasoned that a pet would bring them comfort and that they could provide a safe home for the animal. It was a win-win they all thought. It made sense on a surface level, but many of us in the rescue world worried about when people went back to work what they would do with the newly adopted pet.

We diligently screened applications that came in for animals and made sure people were in it for the long haul...or at least we tried to ensure that as best as we could. In short order, for the first time ever in our history, we adopted out every single cat we had in our rescue and 99% of our dogs.

People were begging for animals to adopt, so I started reaching out to nearby animal control facilities and to other rescue contacts that were fairly close by to see if there were any dogs or cats that needed placement with a rescue. There were absolutely no dogs or cats in need of rescue locally, so I put feelers out farther. I figured that while in northern Illinois we didn't have a huge number of homeless animals there had to still be other areas in the US that had animals in need of rescue.

***

In the animal rescue world, when I first started back in 2003, with the help of modern communication such as the Internet and social media emerging, rescue organizations began collaborating with each other. Rural, impoverished areas where shelters were overrun with homeless animals reached out to rescues and shelters where there were fewer homeless animals. The two very different types of animal rescues partnered together and began transporting animals from the overrun shelters to areas in the US where more adoptions were taking place and there were fewer homeless animals.

Shortly after I started AEAR I was part of the beginning of that new happening between rescue groups and shelters and, as I wrote in my book *The Animal Warrior*, I traveled all over the Midwest visiting rural shelters and rescued and transported animals from southern Illinois, Missouri and Indiana to our area, into foster homes and adopted them out.

But in 2008 I stopped taking animals anymore from outside our area. There were many reasons for this. First of all, I noticed that as all the rescue groups and many shelters in our area kept taking dogs from outside the area, when local animals were in need of a place to go, we were full and couldn't help the local animals. That just didn't seem right. I felt that it was vital for us to concentrate on our local animals. Second, I was concerned about the fact that in taking the animals from places where they didn't spay and neuter their animals and didn't properly care for their animals either we weren't solving any problems but just shifting the problem to us.

The final decision to only rescue local animals came because I was getting majorly burnt out viewing the countless e-mails I received from everywhere with the sad faces of animals. The e-mails begged for the animals' lives to be saved. It was a huge weight I carried just looking at those animals knowing there was no way I could save even a small fraction of the number of animals in need. That in-my-face knowledge with each e-mail I received took a toll on me and I was burning out big time. I had to reel in what I was doing to save my sanity.

But in 2020 with no animals in our care and foster homes willing to take in homeless animals more than ever before I hooked up with a local transport and rescue organization that took dogs and cats from

Tennessee, Kentucky, Arkansas, Indiana and other southern US areas. I received my first e-mail with a list of over 200 dogs and 100 cats that needed places to go.

Looking at all those photos of the faces of the animals and making the decisions about who to take and who not to take brought back memories from the beginning of AEAR and the ups and downs I faced back then. I reminded myself to go forward cautiously and with more wisdom and care for myself. I knew what I was getting into and told myself I would not get to the point of burning out. As soon as things got back to "normal" I would go back to rescuing only locally again.

Jumping back on the that train once again would lead me in a totally new direction and one I never, ever would have thought of. In essence, the upcoming segment of my life in animal rescue would be filled with major ups and downs. But as life works when we lead with an open heart and a passion to help, I would walk down the road to an experience that would change the course of my work and life and that of many other people as well.

***

It was the year 2015. Rounding the curve on the path that circled the lake, ear buds in my ears, the weather was perfect. The sun was warm, the sky clear and I was so very grateful for my life. It had been a year since Chuck's transformation and our lives together were better than ever before. But I still struggled trusting him fully…the enormous and complete change in him…the questions as to why it happened and why now? I continued to be hypersensitive to his everyday actions and reactions to things waiting for "Old Chuck" to reemerge.

But day after day and month after month he continued to show me through his actions the man he had become. For the first time ever I was nurtured, cared for and loved gently and sweetly and in a way that often left me confused and unnerved but also feeling like a special person. I was both relishing in this newfound deep friendship and love and doing all I could to work on myself, forgive him and forgive myself for our past.

By this time in my journey I had taken many classes and certifications in Reiki, past life regression, removing entities, angel work and other healing modalities. After practicing energy healing on many of my friends and getting their feedback I officially opened my company Mindful Spirit and was doing energy healing professionally. I continued to practice enhancing my skills and gifts and was getting great results.

In the past year I studied the concept of "spirit guides" and was fascinated. I loved the idea that guides were all around us helping us. There were different guides that joined us at different points in our lives. I thought it was equally as interesting that there were different types of spirit guides, ones that help with day-to-day tasks, ones that stay with you for a season and ones that are with you for life. It all seemed logical to me too since my whole life I could feel something or somebody around me periodically and it made sense that it was probably my guides.

Through my studies I learned how to tap into the part of my intuition where I was able to meet through my third eye my guides. That was how I communicated with them. It happened most often during meditation that they came through.

My first guide was Danya. Danya helped me receive the messages that nature provided me. All the spirit guides I discovered since then played different roles in my life. Edward helped me to appreciate my physical body. Diane was all about nutrition and wellness. Oliver helped me with technology. Nolan, my most favorite guide, taught me how to have fun again, be playful, learn to trust and even taught me how to fly.

All my guides, up to that moment walking on the trail, were there to help me navigate the day-to-day business of being human in a tough and challenging world. But as I walked on that trail that day what I was still missing was a guide with a broader perspective and a higher vibration whose role was to show me a vision of my place in the world, why I was here and what this all meant for me.

Soft meditation music playing in my ear buds and all my human senses heightened, I entered the All Present space in my mind that opened the door for a higher vibration to come through to my intuition. I felt the warm breeze on my skin, saw the sparkling blue lake, the lush trees and was totally present in that moment. Suddenly I could feel behind my back and along the sides of me something unique.

In my mind's eye I could "see" these softball-sized energy spheres floating behind me and to my back side. At first I was perplexed. Then I just *knew* they were individual souls that were "on the other side," meaning that they were not in human form. But I didn't understand what they were doing around me.

By this time I was used to unusual phenomena happening to me, so I just "watched" them as they followed me as I walked. At the same time I thought of Chuck and myself, our relationship and the incredible shift and change in all of it and asked the Universe, "Why did this happened to us and what is my purpose? Why am I here and why are we together now and as brand new people?"

Suddenly I felt this presence intuitively above my head. I *knew* instantly this was a different kind of guide. I heard: "*You and Chuck are together because you are going to be leading and he is there to support you all along the way. See all the energy around you?*"

"Yes," I answered in my mind.

"*They are all souls that have chosen to follow you, protect you and be with you as you help the world. You are never alone. There are many who will be with you. But we needed a human who could be beside you during this process to help you with Earth-bound goals that we can't do and Chuck made perfect sense. He was and always has been the one to help you. He is also gifted and is an important asset to mankind.*"

"But help me with what? What am I supposed to do?"

"Be you. Spread your light of love. The world needs you and needs it."

"But how?"

"You are doing it now."

"It doesn't feel like it," I said, my heart feeling overwhelmed and heavy.

"Trust the process. You are."

"Who are you?"

"I am a higher guide that helps humanity."

"What is your name?"

"I don't have a human name."

"It's best for me if I have a name so I know how to refer to you."

I could feel this opening up as if he was giving me the okay to see his signature and translate it to English words, and the name Clem came to me. I felt Clem's presence step back and away, but the energy balls around me stayed as I walked. Mystified and feeling an overwhelming sense of love and connection, tears streamed down my face.

Chapter 5

By the spring of 2021 I rescued dozens of dogs and cats through the transport organization and Animal Education and Rescue was in full swing managing the intake of animals. More often than not the animals came to us utterly filthy and with issues. Mud, dirt, urine, feces and who-knows-what else was always coated on their fur. They usually had fleas and ticks. They often had intestinal parasites or another nasty intestinal condition. They sometimes had an upper respiratory infection that caused coughing, runny nose and runny eyes. They sometimes came with eye, ear and skin infections and ear mites. In the summer we took in puppies that came down with parvo, a potentially deadly intestinal virus. We spent a fortune getting them treatment at the animal hospital. It was like we had turned into a full-fledged, emergency, front-lines business for rescue animals.

Most of the dogs and cats were shut down emotionally, confused and basically broken. From the time I chose my first dogs and cats from the e-mail list and until today, as of this writing, it was a long and hard road. So much has changed in the last year and a half…so much.

Spring of 2021 we took in a pregnant dog I named Daisy. She stayed at my house in a penned in area that Chuck had built for dogs in our basement. There she had her puppies. It was perfect for whelping puppies.

It had been a few years since I raised a litter of puppies, so it was an exciting time. I shared the whole experience with our Facebook audience as a means to educate people about raising a litter of puppies. I shared with them every stage of development, as well as the ups and downs of the experience.

Julie, one of my long-time volunteers, was with me for the birth of the puppies. It was her very first time seeing puppies born and watching her enthusiasm and the wonder in her eyes filled my heart with joy. By the time the puppies were six weeks old I was utterly exhausted because I was juggling them and everything else in my life, so when Julie, her daughter Kelsey and their family offered to foster Daisy and her pups the last two weeks, I gratefully took them up on their offer.

The fall of 2021 came and I had enough of a break to forget the hard work of raising a litter of puppies and agreed to once again take in a pregnant dog. This dog we named Robin. I was back on the rollercoaster ride, Julie by my side and our Facebook followers enjoying the adventure.

In the past I tried many ways to gain more followers on Facebook, but we stayed steady with a modest and loyal local following. Every Sunday night I did a "Sunday Night Live" on Facebook where I livestreamed and shared what happened that week at AEAR and what was coming up in the near future. I also did random livestreams on Facebook when we were in the process of doing a rescue or an event or when we took in new animals. Sometimes I did livestreams at foster families' homes to showcase an animal or animals available for adoption. It was typical to get about 20–25 people on our livestreams.

***

Life as we knew it before 2020, when the world shut down, was gone. A new way of navigating life seemed to be the new norm. We didn't know when masks were going to be required in public again; kids in public school were either learning from home or at school with masks. Vaccines became available and people were either scrambling to get them or running away from the mistrust of the shots.

Chuck and I continued to dive deep in learning about the current state of the world, of the vaccines and we were regulars at the meetings put on twice a month by a local health food store.

Being empathic and highly sensitive I mostly stayed in my own happiness bubble and avoided conversations about the virus, the vaccine or anything else political with most people, especially my family and some close friends I knew felt a different way than I did. I knew enough about what was going on to know that fear was incredibly poisonous and I didn't want to take in that toxic energy.

I kept my nose to the ground and did my work and showered myself with healthy lifestyle choices. I spent time in nature, read, meditated, watched inspirational videos and movies, painted, wrote and listened to uplifting music.

I shared the messages of love I had in my heart with my clients and through social media. I knew that love was so powerful and so important. It was vital to people's wellbeing. My work as a spiritual coach and healer was needed more than ever before. Many came to me suffering deeply with debilitating anxiety. People were desperate for relief from their suffering and as I worked with them the progress they made was awe-inspiring.

By this time I was painting almost obsessively and certainly furiously. Some days I completed three paintings! When I painted I got lost in the shades of colors, layers, textures and shapes that manifested and the movement of the paint and water on canvas. Three hours felt like 10 minutes. When I closed my eyes in bed, ready to fall sleep, I saw colors, shapes, designs and textures take shape behind my eyelids.

To my delight my paintings were actually selling, which motivated me to keep doing it. I created a new way of raising money for Animal Education and Rescue…through Chuck's and my artwork! It was exhilarating doing what brought me great therapy and inspiration and helped us continue to make money for AEAR.

***

Gathering in one of the halls of the Akashic Records the Committee gathered into a circle. Mashia began, "Light Ones, have you thought of some way we can help humanity on Earth? I welcome your ideas." The six Wise Ones who volunteered for the committee raised their vibration. A swelling of comradery, admiration and love filled the hall.

Shelke began, "I have spent much time watching the people of Earth and see the pain and suffering everywhere. But in looking deeper within I saw that there are Lightworkers scattered throughout Earth. These humans are without fear and are spreading light where they go. But their Lights of Love seem to be having a hard time reaching through to their fellow humans.

"My conclusion is that they just don't have the power to spread the love because the fear on Earth right now is so dense. As I watch the Lightworkers, I see their energies are being blocked by greater dark forces that have gained power. I also see humans that are young in lifetimes, too weak or are largely unaware that they have any power and light at all. Somehow assist the Lightworkers, to help them extend and grow their Lights' energy and power to reach the humans that are too fearful to see any light at all. The Darkness seems to be taking over."

"It is through the Lightworkers," Layas said. "Human history is such that there have always been Lightworkers and those unique humans have raised their vibrations and assisted humanity to each level of their evolvement."

"Yes," Mashia agreed. "They have come a long way."

"Mashia, Wise Ones, may I?" Danya began quietly. The Committee illuminated their energy in unison. "Thank you," Danya said. "I have been studying the Lightworkers. I know we cannot interfere with individual human or their collective choices. Our laws remain the same, that they must have free will. But I've studied Lightworkers and it seems that at this time they need something to help them get the attention of the others who are weaker. It doesn't seem as if they themselves are enough."

A buzzing of agreement ran through the energies of the Committee.

"As a human of war and destruction would have, say, a gun or a knife, Lightworkers need tools to help them lead the way."

"Yes, my friend, I must agree with that," Shelke said.

"What do you propose from here?" Mashia asked.

"Let me meditate on this, plug into The Collective and we can draw near again in a short while," Danya said.

It was not long until the Committee met again and this time Danya began. "I've meditated, plugged deeply into Source regarding the plight of Earth and the humans on it right now. I have tapped into the Collective, the Wisest of Them All, to bring the highest guidance into my soul. I believe I see clearly what we can do to help without disturbing the human souls' growth or their direction. May I share a vision with you?"

The Committee raised their vibration in unison. Above their light energy fields a projection of Earth appeared before them. Earth began to glow with tiny white lights all over it. "You see the lights? These lights represent the Lightworkers. Their energy fields are struggling and their lights dimly lit. I was told this from The Wisest of them All: 'Humans today have been poisoned with dark energy that is threatening to take over. It is an energy that, over the centuries, has grown larger and stronger. It is the individual souls that over Earth-time and generations chose to walk in the way of anger, hatred, pain and suffering. Their greed has grown and their selfishness is enormous. They have spent so long walking that path that their natural Light of Love is completely unknown by their souls. They are attempting to bring complete darkness onto Earth.

"'Then, as we view Earth from above, we see there are humans that are not exhibiting this intense dark energy, but they are either living as one who Does Not See or are blocked completely by their choosing. It could be from fear and suffering in some, in others not wanting to face courage and others yet whose souls are still young and naive. For this we already know.

"'This has made it very difficult for the Lightworkers on Earth today. They understand that they must light their way with unconditional love, but the powers that are working against them are powerful.'

"Here is what was spoken to me. We set our energy fields to seek out the Lightworkers on Earth today who are not living in fear, souls that have evolved to the stage of development that they can share their messages of love. Then, we utilize the profound healing powers of Earth's animals and the power of nature on Earth to be the tools for which the Lightworkers gain strength and energy and can light the way for others. We can raise our vibrations and plant the seeds for them to tend to and utilize to assist their quest, if they choose. That's all we can do. The rest is up to humanity."

Danya paused and then said, "That is the message I received. We would light our collective energies and rain down that light, wisdom and guidance into and around non-humans, who will serve as conduits to take Earth and its humans to a higher state of growth, healing and to their next stage of evolution."

The room was quiet as each member brought the thought inward. Mashia said, "You have done your homework well, Danya. While we cannot make decisions for Earth or its souls we can assist them to find what they need to do this for themselves. From there, it's up to them. I suggest a vote. Please raise your vibration if you agree that it is the best course of action to send sparks of light down to help guide Earth's humans." The room glowed bright.

Plugging into the Main Collective of Love, the Committee's energetic lights grew brighter, brighter and brighter. Wisdom of the Ages and the Power of Divine Love swelled to such greatness within the hall that an audible buzzing could be heard. Pure, shimmering, spectacular white light magnified larger and larger until a burst of light fractured off and began to move away and down toward Earth. There, individual bits of the All-That-Is-Love penetrated Earth's atmosphere and rained down all around the beautiful blue-green globe, magnetizing toward their intended targets.

One of the droplets of the white lights fell down, down, down to the state of Alabama and to a house of horrors where two dark-energy humans were neglecting dozens of dogs. Animal rescuers were on their way to save them but had yet to arrive. As a speck of light of pure loving energy fell down it was drawn toward a little white-and-brown female dog that was quivering underneath an old, dilapidated porch. The light entered her little body and a glow expanded inside.

Chapter 6

My ring tone indicated a text message came through. Looking at my phone, Lynn, one of the two women who ran the animal transport texted: "There are about 50 dogs that need places. Bad situation. Stupid 'breeder'...NOT! Many dogs pregnant. Can you take any?" That followed with over a dozen of poorly taken photos of dogs in deplorable conditions. Photos were taken clearly in hurry and haste, dogs peeking out of crates, their bodies hunched and eyes big and terribly sad.

"Let me check and see what I can do. What breed/types?"

"Chihuahuas, Jack Russell terriers, Italian greyhound mixes ???? Mixed..."

"Okay. I'll get back to you."

So as I did literally hundreds of times before, I put a plea out on all our social media sites and in e-mails looking for foster homes. To my surprise (because more often than not I don't get any responses initially) I received a response from one of my regular foster moms: "I can take a dog. But I can't take a pregnant dog."

It was more the norm than not that I agreed to take animals without having foster homes lined up for them. If I waited until someone agreed to foster an animal I would be rescuing very few animals. But what I learned after 18 years of trial and error is a method of who to take based on certain factors. The animals have to be able to fit at my house because I never know if and when a foster home will become available, and a foster family can decide at any time to stop fostering and without other options the animal may have to come to my home. In the case of this example we'll focus on dogs, although we take in any kind of domestic pet besides snakes, spiders and farm animals.

The next thing I factor in is what dogs would be more adoptable. While we used to take bully breed dogs we no longer do for many reasons. I consider what dogs we currently have in our care and try and choose dogs that are unlike the ones we currently have so that we have a broad selection…although it isn't a perfect science.

Third, I use my intuition to guide me to the best choices. More often than not we have limited information on the animals and so I am making decisions based on what we do know and what my gut tells me.

The last pregnant dog I took in was Robin, the past October. I fostered her throughout her pregnancy and raising her puppies. It was April of 2022 and I thought I had a decent chance of finding a foster home for a pregnant dog this time, because the dog I was going to take was small, so it would be easier to get a family to commit.

So I banked on only having to keep a pregnant dog for a week or so at my house, optimistic that someone would step up. Not only didn't anyone step up but the decision to take the dog would prove to be a decision that made a much larger impact than I would have ever dreamed possible.

***

April 11, 2022 Lynn arrived at my house with her impressively large animal transport van. She slid the side door open with a loud snap. Staring back at me in over a dozen cages were pathetic-looking dogs crammed in cages with soiled newspaper in disarray in the bottoms and spilling out the sides. The smell, while it had grown familiar to me from the many past transports I had participated in, was overpowering. Dirty, stinky, fear-filled dogs peered wearily at me with saucer-sized eyes telling stories of the pain and suffering they had endured.

"Okay," I sighed, heaviness in my heart for all the dogs, "I can only take three. A pregnant one and I'll take one female that is hopefully not pregnant and I can take one male. That way I know it isn't pregnant. The foster insisted on not getting a pregnant dog," I reminded her (and myself).

"Well, any of these," she pointed at certain cages, "are pregnant for sure. Here's the two males," she pointed at two cages near the bottom.

"Hummm," I scanned the cages, the feeling of sadness for them present in my heart but through conditioning kept at a safe emotional distance. I had a task to do.

"There's more in back." She walked to the back of the truck. I followed her.

She opened up the back and two rows of crates stacked three-high were filled with dogs. "I think all these are pregnant too." I stood there feeling overwhelmed.

"Are they all nice?"

"They are all scared, but only a few are snappy." She pointed at two cages.

"Okay, I can't take those." I knew I couldn't keep Lynn long. She still had many more dogs to place elsewhere, so I peered closer and scanned down to a crate all the way and at the bottom right corner. It was a little white-and-brown dog. Her milk-chocolate brown eyes were big and round and her ears were pulled back. She had cow-like brown patterns, which were adorable. She seemed quite small. "Okay, I'll take this one," I pointed to the dog. "And I'll pick out a male and one that's not pregnant."

Carrying the crates with the dogs I chose inside them, we brought them through the gates to my back yard. I said goodbye to Lynn and she went on to her next stop. Tracy arrived for the male dog and put the dog into her car and left, leaving me with a brindle-colored female dog that looked like a cross between a Chihuahua and an Italian greyhound and the little white-and-brown pregnant dog. They were still in their crates.

"Hi sweeties. It's okay. It's all up hill from here. I promise," I said ever so quietly, looking into each pair of eyes. They looked unsure, but I could see a tiny sparkle of hope yet at the same time.

First, I set up the little brindle dog in the dog room, a room converted from a porch to a fully functioning room utilized for new foster dogs. Because the pregnant dog was small and wouldn't take up a lot of space at the moment I decided to set her up in the middle room on the main floor. That room was being used for storage and was filled high and wide with random supplies. It was, at that moment, a catchall for a lot of stuff. But I made room in one corner for her, figuring it would only be a few days until someone stepped up to foster her.

Settling in her area the little pregnant dog's eyes followed me as I busied myself getting her food, water, pee pads and a dog bed. I also gave her an assortment of toys. She was very untrusting of me and slinked back when I approached too closely. I had fostered enough terrified dogs to know that I needed to give her time and space. She would come around.

That night on my livestream on Facebook I introduced the pregnant dog. "This little dog came in earlier today and she's very pregnant. I'm setting her up in this area temporarily, hoping that a foster home becomes available." Then, as I often do, I talked directly to the little dog, "Don't worry, girlfriend. You are safe with me and I'll take care of you. You will have nothing to fear from here forward. You may not know it yet, but I do love you very much."

The following day Dawn, one of my volunteers,

stopped by to pick up some supplies she needed. She walked into the storage room where I was spending some time with the dog and remarked, "Oh, she's adorable!" The dog scooted past Dawn to avoid getting too close. "Oh, look," Dawn pointing at the dog, "she has a flower on her back." I looked closely at the pattern on the dog's back and sure enough there was a little brown flower surrounded by white fur on her upper left backside. "Oh, yeah, I see it." Inspired by that, I named the little white-and-brown dog Flower.

Meanwhile life continued as usual. Chuck and I were working at our usual high speed, juggling our daily businesses. A few days later I received a text from Lauren, a 23-year-old woman I have known since she was eight years old: "Can I come to help take care of the puppies?"

"Sure," I answered.

"Can I stay with you?"

"Yes, you can."

"Okay, I'll let you know when I get my flight."

Lauren joined Animal Education and Rescue's youth club when she was eight years old. She was very enthusiastic about the club from the start. She quickly grew close to me and was the most active youth club member I had. She tagged along with me to all the events the youth club members were invited to and every single field trip we put on. Sometimes she came back to my home to hang out with us or to share a meal.

Lauren was the oldest of three adopted children, raised by a single mother. As a fellow adoptee I felt a special kinship to her. I also loved Lauren's tenderness and sensitivity to people and animals. She was and is a girl in some ways just like me—highly sensitive and empathic toward people and toward animals.

Throughout the years Lauren continued to be involved with AEAR's youth club and aged out of the club at 18 but stayed on as a volunteer. By that time I knew that Lauren was intellectually delayed, but other than my observations from spending time with her and the little that her mom shared, I wasn't aware of the day-to-day details of her challenges.

In 2018 Lauren began spending more time at my house, helping out and spending time with us. We were very much like a second family to her and I loved her like a daughter. Danny and Lauren were also very much like siblings. It was nice for Danny, who is being raised as an only child, to have someone in his life that was like a sibling to him.

Occasionally Lauren spent the night and I'd find her the next morning with a few of the dogs cuddled contently around her. She began talking about how her mom was going to be moving to another state and that she didn't want to move with her. For over a year periodically Lauren would ask if she could live with us permanently and each time I told her that I needed to speak to her mother about it.

She always replied that she knew that and that her mother would contact us. That went on for so long

I finally texted her mother about Lauren's desire to live with us. She did not respond. It was very frustrating. I wasn't comfortable telling Lauren she could live with us until I had a better understanding of what her special needs were and what we would have to do for her on a regular basis. It was a big commitment and we wanted to make sure it was something we could manage.

Five days before her mother was scheduled to move to Maine, Lauren called me and said, "I'm moving into your house in a few days."

Once again I told her that her mother had never contacted me and that I needed to speak to her. Long story short her mom and I had a brief conversation at which time she told me that she would me call back in a few hours to schedule a time for us to speak further. An hour later I received a text from Lauren saying, "I'm moving with my mom to Maine." Lauren moved to Maine in the winter of 2021.

Chapter 7

Our home has served us well since we moved here in 1993. It's housed our family and many businesses throughout the years. Built in 1910, it's long and box-shaped with many small rooms on all three floors. Thanks to Chuck's skills as a handyman the house has morphed into many different internal shapes as our lives and our businesses needed it.

When we first moved here, my long-time business The Pet Sitters of America was run out of a room in our basement. Then there was a period of three years that we expanded our business and offered dog grooming. We moved the whole business to 1,000 square feet of space in a strip mall.

After our lease was up we moved the businesses back home. In preparation for the move Chuck built a wall that separated the house essentially in two halves, side by side. His dog grooming and our two offices were on one side and our living quarters were on the other side, as well as upstairs. The basement was used for storage but often had water seepage, so it was not as functional as we would have liked it to be.

It's been so many years and there have been so many changes I can only remember the major ones. How it stands now is that has Chuck built walls right through the whole center length of the house to accommodate AEAR. Volunteers can come in and out of the house and do what they need to do without disturbing our personal space. As long as people don't enter through doors that say, "Please do not enter," we can move around freely and have our privacy. Supplies for AEAR fill our garage, two sheds and are scattered throughout the house. Animals come and go from our home as they are rescued and either go to foster homes or get adopted.

My yellow and white 1966 *Decamp* trailer is located in our driveway just behind the house. It's truly my most favorite place. It's where I see clients for energy healing and spiritual coaching. It's a space where we sometimes complete adoptions and where meetings take place. I also meditate in it regularly and it's a great getaway if I just need a break from the animals. We even have meals in there sometimes.

The back part of the driveway has been converted to a giant outdoor play area for the dogs and the back yard (grassy area), separated by a six-foot stockade fence, is an even bigger play area. The dogs get to romp in the grassy yard periodically, but because of the damage they cause to the grass it's regulated.

We live in a very urban-like suburban area beside a busy road. On either side of our property there is a church, a school and a doctor's office. It gets very loud during school days. Every year the church has a pig roast, which we dread because as vegetarian, animal-lovers, the smell of cooking flesh right next to our fence turns our stomachs. Last year they dumped the grease from the pig roast right up against our fence. Our dogs were obsessed with that area…ugh!

Easter our neighbors put up a makeshift cave out

front of their church where people dress up as guards to Jesus. It's a creative expression of waiting for Jesus to arrive. They stand guard all night long before Easter Sunday and we can hear horns honking that night as cars pass by and the people wave at the guards. The church is a very creative bunch!

We have made do with what we have carved out for ourselves, and it's been a very interesting life and lifestyle, but we have always longed for more land, some privacy and a bigger space. We've looked at properties on and off throughout the years, but the perfect property and the cash necessary to do it hasn't presented itself. So we are and remain grateful that our humble house has provided so much love and safety to so many animals and has created jobs for us and others and that we've served our communities. Our home is safe, warm and the very center of our world.

***

One day, shortly after Flower arrived Nikki and I were sitting in the trailer talking. She came over periodically to get supplies for her foster kittens, to help out with the animals or to help organize the endless supplies that arrived and needed sorting. Getting to know Nikki I felt like we really complemented each other. Our core values were the same but our skills and talents quite different. Chatting I said something that I had said once before to her, "I sure wish I could hire you to help me."

She smiled and nodded.

"I know," I went on, "you have a good job at the animal hospital."

"Yes, I do. If I didn't it would be different. But they really need me there."

"I know," I agreed. "I couldn't afford you anyway," I shrugged and smiled.

Typically once a day or so, I did livestreams on Facebook at all different times, sharing with my modest audience what was going on with AEAR. At the moment the big news was the very pregnant dog we had in our storage room. She was getting so big that the poor girl looked like she was going to pop!

Some things were changing noticeably around me. It wasn't more than a week or so since Nikki and I spoke about her job that things started falling apart for her there. Lauren would be arriving to help with the puppies at the beginning of May. Chuck and I, as usual, were juggling a million things at once: our businesses, our son Danny, our household and all the animals that were with us. Life was chaotic, but that was nothing new for us until something completely new turned things upside down.

It was a Tuesday night and I was doing a livestream on Facebook showing everyone on the live a very pregnant Flower, who was just going about doing what dogs do, when suddenly I started seeing comments that got my attention. "Hello Mary from the UK! Hi M Ann Marie from Ohio! Hello there Tina from Australia!"

Within an hour our Facebook page blew up with people coming on from all over the world: the UK, Australia, New Zealand, South Africa, all over the US and more. I sat there watching the comments and names scroll, open-mouthed and in shock. As people said hello, I said hello back and I called out what state or country they were tuning in from out loud. "Okay, well, I can't believe we are getting people from all over," I said, "but welcome to our page." I shook my head in bewilderment. It felt as if I had opened up my home to the world…and in essence I had.

That night I sat at my living room table, the dogs all snoozing or relaxing around me and I went back to the livestream from earlier in the evening. I scrolled back to the beginning and wrote down on a piece of paper a list of where everyone was tuning in. I was near tears by the end, my heart exploding in my chest. *What is happening here?*

Flower Power and her Buds!
Love and Support from _Love is the answer_
around the world!

Scotland
Montana
Barbados
Washington State
Belfast
Canada
Liverpool UK
Wales
Norway
Swindon in UK
Wisconsin, USA
Rochester, NY USA
N. Ireland
Scotland
Louisiana USA
England
San Diego
UK
Texas USA
Newcastle, UK
Netherlands
Ashtabula, Ohio USA
Portage, Michigan
Arizona USA
Tennessee, USA
Lake in the Hills, Il. USA
Holland, Europe
Georgia
Quebec, Canada
Virginia, USA
Nashville USA

South Wales, UK
Pennsylvania USA
West Wales
South Africa
UK
South Wales
England
Ohio, USA
Crystal LK, Fl.
Alabama, USA
Upstate NY
Lake George, NY
Scotland
Oklahoma
N.E. England
Iowa, USA
Stoke
Shropshire, England
Switzerland
N. Carolina
New York USA
Scotland
Delray Beach, Fl.
Oregon
NJ
Maryland
Kentucky
Belfast
Canada

Stockport UK
Louisiana
Kentucky
Canada
Albuquerque, NM
Finland
Rhode Island
Staffordshire, England
Baja Norte, Mexico
Oklahoma)
New Brunswick, Canada
California
England
St. Charles, Il.
Eastbourne in UK
New Jersey
Morris, Illinois
Fresno, Canada
SW Utah.
Missouri
Petersburg, H.
UK
France
South Port, Merseyside UK

Nikki and I spoke almost daily and in just a few short days her job became so toxic that she quit. I said to her, "Come and work for me for 90 days. I can commit to that, not more right now. But I need the help and you need a job. And who knows maybe we can figure out how to keep you on permanently." Without hesitation she agreed. I encouraged her to take a week off to decompress after a really rough time at her previous place of employment. Reluctantly she agreed.

The following morning I went about my daily chores and the day began as usual. That evening I did another livestream, sure that the night before was a fluke. But there it went again, people flooded onto my screen and into our cyber-home. "Hello Jamie from Newcastle in the UK. Welcome Jennie from Scotland. Hi Marianne from Louisiana…" and so it went and I just rolled with it, as one might do if receiving unexpected guests. I just welcomed them into my home.

The next few days messages started coming through on my Facebook page's messenger. People offered advice on how to properly do livestreams: "Do livestreams twice a day." "You should set up a tripod and just let it livestream. Then when the puppies are born just let people watch for an hour or so. You can leave and come back if you have to." A third person said, "I'm going to buy you a tripod." Within 48 hours I had three tripods and a selfie stick from various people arrive in packages at my front door.

Chapter 8

With hundreds of Facebook followers now watching us daily I was flooded with comments and a lot of busy-body, back-seat-driver behavior. I was spending many hours every day answering the dozens of questions or comments that came through. I was putting out fire after fire where people misinterpreted a photo, post or video they saw and I'd have to clarify what was really happening.

It just boggled my mind that so many people would automatically draw conclusions about things based on very little information. Emotions on Facebook were high and I kept trying to be kind and courteous and respond to the flurry of communication. This was all new to me and in short order things got really rough for a while.

Every day for weeks I shared Flower on Facebook on livestreams, in photos and videos. All around the world we were waiting, holding our breaths, for the big day and she just got bigger and bigger and bigger.

April 23, 2022 Flower finally went into labor. She was a nervous dog that had finally learned to trust me and Nikki but nobody else. That day she was fussy and fidgety and wouldn't settle down. The baby pool I put in her space as her whelping box wasn't satisfying her. Baby pools were what I always used. I remembered from past experiences that a cardboard box turned sideways sometimes worked well to create a cave-like environment for them. So I grabbed a box and sure enough that did the trick.

Nikki was with me that day and we waited and waited for Flower to have her puppies and nothing was happening, but we knew based on her behavior she was in labor. Finally it was dinnertime and Chuck wasn't home, so I had to feed the dogs dinner. I told Nikki I would be back in a few minutes and that she was on puppy watch. Fortunately Flower had grown somewhat used to Nikki, so I felt confident I could leave for a short while.

Hurriedly I busied myself preparing all the dogs' food bowls. Just as I finished I heard, "Sandy, Sandy…" It was Nikki frantically trying to find me in the house…the house was like a maze with a million doors. Nikki told me later that she watched as Flower's first puppy was born and it plopped on the ground and was still surrounded in its slimy, bloody sack. Not knowing what to do Nikki reached over and picked up the sticky puppy in its sack and looked at Flower who looked back at her like, *I have no clue what to do; you figure this out.* Panic setting in, that's when Nikki gently put the puppy back down near Flower and ran to get me.

Hustling into the room I bent down close into the dark box where Flower was curled up and looked at the puppy. Flower was licking the puppy and had removed the sack. Two more puppies were born in four hours. Peering into the box we were relieved to see that the puppies were cleaned up and curled up by mom, suckling. It seemed that Flower was getting the hang of this motherhood thing. Flower made it clear that she did not want any help from us and we were fairly confident if we got too close she might nip us.

Eventually Nikki went home and by the next morning eight puppies were delivered from that tiny 12-pound Flower. I marveled that so many pups had been inside of her. I kept going back into the room to check on them. Looming in close I adjusted my eyes to the darkness in the box and counted them over and over again. Snuggled so close and intermeshed it wasn't easy to see each pup individually. They just looked like one big clump of wiggly, cooing tiny puppies. The whole time I was posting videos, doing livestreams and posting photos of the family on Facebook and our audience continued to grow.

By this time Facebook was becoming a full-time job. I was constantly on the page fielding questions and comments and trying to be nice but getting stressed out from the constant and persistent back-seat drivers. A few days after Flower had her puppies I received two messages on Facebook messenger from people that were criticizing everything I was doing and bashing my character and everything about me. They were clearly written by disturbed individuals. It really scared me and I realized in that moment that I was in a very vulnerable and potentially dangerous situation. I quickly deleted the messages and blocked the people, but it unnerved me to the core.

Meanwhile I was receiving private messages on Facebook from other people as well. There were many that were kind and encouraging and praising me for my work. One of the people was a woman named Peggie who quickly began to observe the comments I was receiving and offered suggestions and encouragement about them. In short order we struck up a kind of friendship and she began watching the page even closer.

Someone else, seeing how frantic the page was becoming with all the nosy comments and my responses messaged me and told me that I need to assign people to monitor my page. They said that I need someone other than myself, which made total sense to me at that point since between taking care of Flower and the puppies, all the other animals, Danny, my other company and everything else I do in a day I was being swallowed up by Facebook. On livestreams, the comments scroll by so quickly that I often missed many of them. So I started looking for someone to help me monitor the page.

Peggie, my new advocate, gave me advice on what to do should I receive any more hateful and angry messages: "Take a screen shot and report it to Facebook. If it seems threatening to you personally go to the police and file a report." My heart was so heavy that night that we had to have that conversation at all. I questioned whether I should continue the Facebook page as it was or discontinue posting anything about Flower and her puppies. It seemed like people were getting very emotionally attached to the story that was unfolding and attention was very much on every single move I made. I wouldn't have minded so much because I have nothing to hide, but the misconstrued assumptions and perceptions was constant and I just didn't know how to fix the problem.

The next morning, still numb and sad by the toxic messages I received, what was happening on my Facebook page, as well as feeling consumed by the workload of managing Facebook, I decided to do a special livestream where I talked about it.

Taking a deep breath I opened my heart and pushed the blue LIVE button on my phone, the camera facing me. "Hello everyone," I began, more somber than my usual chipper self. "This live is an important one and I want to make sure you are all listening in." I could see that people were jumping on our page. The numbers were climbing...25, 26, 65... When I got to 100 people I began, "Okay, here's where we are everyone and I want to be very clear. I am very grateful for all of the support I've been receiving. And if you are new to us you are still getting to know me and us. I totally understand that.

"Here's the thing, everyone. I have received two very cruel and scary messages from people on private messenger that were uncalled for and untrue. I have blocked them. I am also monitoring this page very closely and having to answer so many questions that really, many of them are not people's business. I've been running this business for close to 20 years, so I must be doing something right if I'm still doing it today. The relentless questioning of everything I do and everything you see and me feeling like I need to respond to everything is taking up, literally, all my time.

"Some of the mean-spirited comments and the ignorant statements are wearing me down." Then, in a firm and stern voice, peppered with a tough-love tone I said, "I've got this. I can handle this. I don't need your help on everything. I will ask when I want help, I promise. But I've got this and you have to let me do my job."

With that a flood of hearts, cares and thumbs up emojis rained down my cell phone screen along with a long line of comments:

"We trust you"

"I know you've got this!"

"You're doing great!"

"I love what you do" …and so many more.

Looking at the flood of hearts and thumbs up and words of encouragement I smiled warmly and took a breath. "Thank you for the kindness. That's what I need right now, your support." Then pausing and putting on my best-determined face I said, "But if the negativity or the bossiness or negative assumptions continue I will not think twice about not sharing anything anymore. I won't be treated badly in my own home. Just think of it this way."

I went on, "Imagine that you are in my home, really physically in my home, that we are seeing each other face-to-face. Think about what you say…'would I say that to her face in her own home?' If the answer is no, then don't do it. If you have a question or comment that if you were in my home you would ask me privately, then you can message me privately."

The flood of emojis expressed their support and their feelings. That live created a pivotal change for our Facebook page. I drew a hard line and people all over the world rallied around me and became more and more faithful and protective of me. Over time I created a way in which I began and ended each Facebook livestream. It went like this: "Good morning (or evening) everyone! This is Sandy Kamen Wisniewski with Animal Education and Rescue. Welcome! We will wait until people get on board."

Then I would watch the comments and as they scrolled by people would say hello and I would say hello back to them, "Hello Vicky from the UK," "Sally, hello! South Africa," until I had 100 people on. Then I would say, "Welcome to my home and our page. All kind, loving, caring, evolving people from all over the world are welcome here."

Over some time I added to that, "If anyone is new to us we welcome you and if you feel so inclined, tell us who you are and where you are from. If there is anyone on here that is suffering in any way right now, know we are wrapping you up in love. And if there is anyone on now that has a tendency to say inappropriate things or bully people on Facebook you are welcome to stay on if you stay silent. If you or anyone else says things that are not appropriate or are mean your comment could be deleted or you could be banned. We play nicely on this playground."

To wrap up the live I always end with, "This is Sandy with Animal Education and Rescue spreading love, joy, education and inspiration around the world."

In the beginning when we received worldwide followers someone messaged me on Facebook and said, "You need to put a donate button on your page for livestreams." I had no idea what they were talking about, but they insisted that it will "take your non-profit to the next level. You could get regular donations that way. And I'm sure you could use the money." I couldn't believe these random people coming out of the woodwork, complete strangers, offering suggestions to help us that way. Never before had this happened. Within 24 hours I figured out how to add the donate button and on the next live we raised close to $1,000. I was totally shocked. *Maybe I can keep Nikki on… Maybe things are really changing…*

Chapter 9

The puppies were two days old and Flower was still very leery of anyone going near her and her pups. I could gingerly navigate around her. The morning of the third day I received this message on Facebook: "I don't want to alarm you, but I was looking at a video you posted and I think one of the puppies doesn't have front legs."

By then I was so used to people seeing things negatively, wrongly and dramatically on all my posts and videos. I responded: "It's very dark in the box and the videos are also grainy. I'm sure it's just the angle." But as soon as I finished typing I went into the puppy room and peered in close to the puppies gathered around Flower's teats and began to gently and cautiously move each one, examining them closely. Looking at the third puppy, the smallest, I saw…the puppy had no front legs. My heart dropped. *Oh no, what am I going to do now?*

Later that day I posted a photo on Facebook of the puppy without front legs and shared how I was very concerned for the puppy and that "we would do the best we could for the puppy, but some things are out of our control." I explained that we'd have to see how she develops and we would do everything we could. Shockingly and to my dismay some people took that as meaning that we might consider putting her to sleep and they said some totally inappropriate comments such as, "How could you say that? She's a live animal and should be given as much of a chance." "What are you SAYING?????" and so forth. It was ridiculous. The outrageous comments warranted some of those people getting blocked and others received a stern warning and a suggestion that they really READ what I wrote and not jump to negative conclusions.

In the next post I wrote about the puppy I sternly told people they need to stop thinking the worst of me and that, "I GOT THIS." In the following livestream I repeated myself. It felt like I was dealing with a bunch of teenagers or kids and that they were in a playground and I was the playground monitor. It was exhausting, but I was growing more accustomed to dealing with the way things were on Facebook and each day I seemed to be able to control the masses, finding a balance of being loving and being firm.

As I write this, on the other end of this story I've asked myself dozens of times why I put up with all of it and why I just didn't stop posting. It was because the positive always outweighed the negative, and I had a deep knowing that this was supposed to play out and it was leading me to a deeper meaning and purpose in life.

***

When the puppies were four days old Nikki started working for AEAR part time. I asked her to take photos of all the puppies and told her that we had to name them. There were two brown puppies, one with a tiny spot of white between his shoulders and one brown puppy with a lot of white on her chest. The rest were like Flower, white all over with big brown patches in varying shapes and sizes. Their markings reminded me very much of cow markings. A few pups had blue eyes and a few had one blue eye and one brown eye.

To honor the volunteers who had helped at that time I let them each name a few puppies. We all decided they would be flower-type names. So there was blue-eyed Lotus (first born), a white and brown female; Basil, the brown one with a tiny bit of white on his shoulder blades and one blue eye and one brown eye; Sweet Pea, the big brown one with white on her chest; Clover, a white pup with two large circles of brown on his back; Fennel, a brown pup with a stripe down his spine of a slight variation of brown and one blue and one brown eye; Lily, a white pup with brown markings; Sprout, a stoutly guy with bright blue eyes; and Blossom, who I named, the tiniest pup, white with brown patterns, dark, dark brown eyes and with only two legs.

The first three weeks were fairly uneventful for Flower and what I began calling "her buds," except for the challenges we faced with Blossom. The rest of the buds drank and slept. Flower cleaned up after them. Our job at that time was to make sure Flower was doing her job and also to tend to Flower's needs. Puppies need to be stimulated to pee and poop by their mom licking their rear ends (and she licks it up...I know, gross...but it's true). Nikki weighed them the three days a week she was there and their weights were slowly climbing...all but Blossom's weight. She seemed to be stuck at the weight she was, gaining very little.

Born with only the senses of smell and touch puppies army-crawl/swim instead of walk. Their main mission is to get to mom for milk and to snuggle close to mom and the other puppies for warmth. At two weeks the pups began winking at us, where their eyes began to open. I love that stage because it seems like when they finally see us they are like, "Wow, what is this?" Their ears began to resemble puppy ears and they could hear. By three weeks old they could all see and hear. Shortly they would begin toddling around like little tipsy windup toys.

From time the puppies are born and until they are eight weeks old, when hopefully they get adopted, there are vast changes and the time in one sense goes by quickly and on the other hand seems so tenuous and painstakingly slow.

After the first stage, which typically is the easiest for us humans and the hardest for mom, the next stage begins with the dog mom no longer cleaning up after the puppies. The area where the puppies live becomes a place where every time you walk in there's poo and pee everywhere.

The more mobile the puppies get the more excited they get to see their human caretakers when they enter the room. Then it's a race to see how fast you can clean the mess as the puppies step all in it and jump all over you getting poo and pee everywhere. Let me tell you they poo and pee a lot. If you ever see a video of a cute pile of puppies playing in a spotless area I promise it's because they just cleaned it before filming.

***

From the very start I was keeping a protective eye on Blossom. She was one-third the size of her littermates and seemed so fragile compared to the others. She was using her tiny back legs to scoot between her littermates to get to her mom's milk, which was encouraging. Luckily, she was tenacious from the get-go, driven to survive by bulldozing up and over, under or in between the littermates. She was determined to live. But by the age of just shy of three weeks, even a very determined pup like Blossom was getting squished by her littermates, who were growing twice as fast as she was.

Another worry for me was that for the first few weeks, periodically, Flower would remove Blossom from her pile of puppies when I wasn't there and put her on the other side of the room. I'd come in with Blossom wiggling and crawling around trying to find her family. A few times Flower also removed Clover from the pile and I'd find both pups somewhere else in the room.

Of course I'd put them back with mom and have a little talk with Flower telling her that what she was doing was not acceptable even if she thinks it is. I was perplexed as to why she removed Clover (he was growing and developing normally and was healthy), but in regards to Blossom, it was obvious. Animals will set aside "imperfect" or "sickly" offspring to concentrate on the healthy ones.

By the time the puppies were three weeks old Blossom was no longer able to get to mom's milk at all no matter how hard she tried…and believe me she had chutzpah. The last straw was the day I walked into the room and had to pull her out from underneath all her littermates. So I began bottle-feeding her full time, except the rare times I could put her on Flower's belly after her littermates had their fill. It was an exhausting three weeks of very little sleep for me.

Carrying Blossom and holding her was very nerve-wracking for me because of my tremor. For decades I was ashamed of my tremor and hid my hands. I cursed the shaking and the handicap it caused me. But now I see the tremor as a blessing in disguise. Because of my tremor I am reminded to take care of myself everyday otherwise suffer the consequences, and I certainly need to be able to use my hands every day!

But the lack of sleep and workload I was experiencing at that time, when Blossom was three weeks old, I had no control over. Picking up that tiny 10-ounce puppy and carrying her and managing the feedings was hard for me. But I managed. It felt like every time I carried her and fed her it was like carrying around a very wiggly raw egg. She certainly was about the same size.

***

Here's a message I received from a Facebook follower:

"I have watched since Flower was pregnant. I love seeing the changes in Blossom and how she is truly blooming under the glow of your love and care. I truly enjoy seeing all of your babies and seeing them grow and change.

The work you do is truly amazing. Seeing the strength in Blossom and all the pups gives me hope. I, myself, have been through some really hard times in the last few years.

Blossom and all of the fur babies give me something good to look forward to every day, especially on my darkest days when PTSD threatens to take me under for the final time. If all of them can keep fighting to live so can I.

Thank you for all you do."
— Rebecca L.

Here's what someone else said:

"I was feeling very low and came across your page, don't actually know how. I watched from the start Flower and pups and when you told us Blossom had no front legs I was hooked.

That little pup puts a smile on my face every day. I am addicted to the page and smile every time I watch your videos. My mood changes after seeing the pups and I can just imagine getting a cuddle from them.

So thank you for helping them, but thank you also for helping me. xx"
— Gail B.

Chapter 10

One of the big tasks that had to be done was to clean the storage room and then, following that, the basement. The storage room was filled with supplies on shelves, in containers and piles everywhere. It was a mess.

The basement, which was unfinished with cement floors and walls, at one point in the home's history was used possibly as a recreation room. That was long ago and changed to walls with broken paneling, partial drywall and some bare cement walls. It was far from pretty, but there were high ceilings and big windows. Thanks to Chuck's hard work water no longer seeped in when it rained. The basement has been used since Chuck fixed the water seepage to temporarily house many animals on and off throughout the past three years or so.

The basement was a catchall for a huge variety supplies. With our constant go-go-go and the in and out of donations the basement was very disorganized and stuff was in piles and heaps everywhere. Nikki set to the task of cleaning and organizing everything. She was fantastic at it and thrived on the hard work and the challenge.

The people following us on Facebook watched every move we made and were constantly sharing advice and warnings. From the start we were instructed that the space where Flower was staying was hazardous. I had to remind them over and over again that she was there temporarily until we could find a foster home and that it was fine for now. Then when we didn't find a foster home I had to show them that we were cleaning the space so they'd stop bugging me about it.

At the same time all our new social media "parents" commented on the exposed wires that "puppies can chew" and "they need to be covered." The pups weren't even BORN yet! I had to keep reminding them that the wires would be covered before the puppies began running around. When that time came I made sure that I posted a photo of Chuck working on covering the wires so they'd stop pestering us about it. Oh, and about the blankets, "Flower needs a blanket" in the baby pool we were using as a whelping box. It was at least a dozen times in a few days I had to tell them that Flower digs and removes the blanket. But that didn't seem to satisfy the masses, so I kept putting a towel or blanket in the pool anyway, even though she pushed it aside.

Let's not forget too the people saying NOT to put a towel or blanket in the pool because "the pups could suffocate." People began voicing their opinion that they didn't like the baby pool as a whelping box even though I told them that we always used a pool in the past and it worked out fine. I tried over and over to tell people that I knew what I was doing. I said, "We've raised dozens of litters and I've been doing this for 20 years. You have to trust me on this. We got this."

Like magic a real whelping box arrived at our door. A woman on Facebook bought it. I knew by then that many people were being bossy but they cared very much. Then when someone decided the whelping box wasn't big enough they bought us an extension to the whelping box we had.

So many well-meaning people were such a blessing but also incredibly exhausting. Their constant needling added onto the stress from everything else I was juggling and managing. They were the true definition of helicopter parents!

All the outpouring of concern, love and attention around the world was humbling, awesome and exhausting. I was trying to balance everything that was going on between social media, the effects of our newfound attention and everything else in my life. I had waves of deep frustration with all the bossiness and righteousness and grappled with how to deal with it. Some of the new regulars who "got it" told me to just ignore all the negative or instructive comments, but I knew from running a social media presence for a long time that ignoring people could only make things worse.

So over time I devised a plan. I came up with some phrases that served me well. One was, "This is not my first rodeo. I've been at this nearly 20 years." Another was, "We got this." Then I encouraged regular followers to back me up and respond to new people with the answers they sought so I didn't have to always answer them. Like if someone said, "You need to have blankets in the baby pool," a follower would answer for me, "No, Flower digs them out. She likes the bottom of the pool as-is."

Figuring out how to utilize our Amazon wish list proved to be extremely helpful. As soon as we put anything on there that we needed it would get purchased and be at our front door. People were scrambling to purchase things for the growing dog family, really begging us to come up with something they could buy for them. Packages sometimes were stacked so high at the front door that we couldn't get inside the door.

Private messages on Facebook came pouring in from people sharing how happy they were to find us and from people offering advice. I started getting letters in the mail from people who said that watching Flower and her pups had greatly improved their lives and it gave them something positive to look forward to.

"I was so depressed 'cause my mom's health was bad and I didn't know what to do, until one day on Facebook I came across the video of Flower and her buds.

Well, I noticed Blossom and I saw how with all her disabilities she was determined to live and nothing was gonna stop her. She was my rock and still is.

I almost gave up 'til I saw that little puppy fight to live. To this day I'm so in awe with how nothing is

gonna stop her. She gave me the strength and hope of not giving up. She is an amazing little pup. Her name is true, "small but mighty."
— Tammy P.
Olive Branch, Mississippi

***

At the time Flower first came into our care people began to learn more about our family and most especially me. I'm a very transparent person and believe that in that authenticity I can best help others. I am what I am and have no pretenses. I also love telling stories, so as each livestream "rolled" and the viewers watched the puppies each day I told stories. I shared funny stories, serious stories, told them about my day and what we were doing. I educated them along the way, spread inspiring messages and overall loved each and every one of them.

Social media can be good or bad, depending on how you navigate it. I've known that fact for as long as I've used it. It's just like real life, no different. So early on I set up strong boundaries with my followers and Peggie and Trudy, my two very faithful and dedicated monitors, ensured people played nice on our page.

***

When the pups were about a week old I got sick.

It started with this deep pain in my bones like my bones were made of glass. By that afternoon I was in bed. My bedroom was upstairs about 35 steps from Flower, her pups and most especially Blossom. I had Nikki three days a week during the day and a few volunteers coming and going helping out a few hours every day. Lauren had not arrived to help yet. So I forced myself out of bed to tend to the puppies, but my energy was zero and I began spiking a fever.

I continued doing two livestreams a day and tending to Facebook. I also had everything else I was responsible for accomplishing daily, things that nobody but me could do. It was too much and I became weepy, emotional and weaker. Fueled by the fever I worried nonstop about the puppies. I was trying so hard to will the illness away, but my body was deciding something else. It was telling me *you must rest.* My fever spiked to 102.3 and I was done, in bed, unable to get up.

At that point I delegated all responsibilities to Chuck, Nikki and Julie. Julie came by three to four times a week for a few hours each time (at least from what I remember from a foggy brain). Chuck and Nikki stepped up their game and the puppies were in good care.

The pain in my bones was excruciating, so I was taking a painkiller and fever reducer. I very rarely take medicine, so that tells you how sick I was. At one point I said to Chuck and Julie separately, "If I die I'm sorry I left such a mess for you." Chuck knows I can be melodramatic at times, especially on the rare occasions I am sick, so he brushed it off. But Julie…well, I frightened her. I surmised this when her response was, "Sandy, you are scaring me." Quickly realizing my mistake I followed up with, "Oh, I'm sure I'll be fine."

No, I would NOT see a doctor unless I was suffering so badly I couldn't manage myself. I'm not one to see doctors unless I really, really have to and it was not gonna happen. I believe in self-healing first and foremost. I knew I would kick it and if it got really, really bad maybe I'd seek help. Dear reader, you may not agree with me, but accept it as it was. This is how I live my life. Fortunately the day after I thought I was on death's door, with lots of herbal supplements and water, monitoring my temperature and staying in bed, rest (sort of) and self-healing I slowly got better. It was a rough week for all of us.

Two-and-a-half weeks old and the puppies' eyes were opening and they were beginning to wobble about trying to find their walking legs. Sometimes I put Blossom on Flower's teat if there was room, or if not I fed her. But I made sure she drank every three hours. She was pooping and peeing sometimes on her own on a pee pad that I used in her "changing table."

Blossom's changing table was a clear box (no lid) I had on a table. My helicopter parents on Facebook expressed concern that even though there was no lid on the changing table they were complaining about ventilation, so to appease them I had a volunteer drill holes all over the sides.

Her little body system worked like a well-run machine. She drank and then she peed and about four times a day she pooped. She was very clean and always pooped and peed on her pad. As soon as she peed or pooped, she would hop/scoot away from the mess. I was impressed and boasted that Blossom was a very smart little pup and was actually nearly housebroken.

***

"One day I was really down and depressed and I came upon your story about Flower and her buds on Facebook. I started watching every day and she brought joy into my life once again.

There's not one day I don't miss watching your livestream. Animal Education and Rescue and staff, you guys are amazing. And I feel the love and joy from each and every one when I watch you work with all the beautiful fur babies. Keep up the good work."
— Teresa B.
Amarillo, Texas

***

Periodically I put Blossom with her dog family so that she had the warmth and companionship of her siblings and her mom, but the robust and wiggly crew quickly crowded her out or piled on top of her. I was always hovering right there and quickly removed her from under a pile of puppies or from underneath mom. She was less than one pound to their three pounds. Mom was at a svelte 14 pounds.

Blossom's eyes seemed to be bulging out more than the other puppies' and her head seemed more apple-shaped than the rest of them. Something seemed off. I remembered taking in a puppy a year before with a condition called hydrocephalus. It's an affliction where there is a buildup of cerebrospinal fluid in a dog's brain. The fluid builds up, placing pressure on the brain, which can lead to brain damage and even death. Considered a congenital disease, that means a dog is born with hydrocephalus. The puppy we took in the year before died a horrible death. It was heartbreaking.

After a few Facebook followers also expressed concern over the shape of her eyes and head and suggested she might have hydrocephalus I decided to make an appointment at the vet. I reminded everyone that there was no sense in worrying and instead we should be sending positive energy and good vibes. But the appointment was 10 days away. That's not unusual these days. Getting into a vet sometimes takes weeks. It's a HUGE dilemma and a problem we still face every day.

Blossom continued to eat like a champ and was hitting her own unique milestones, as were her littermates. They were all slowly developing their own little personalities. By four weeks, Clover, the biggest at that point, somehow managed to climb out of the whelping box when I wasn't there and when I came in was really quite proud of himself. His little chest was pumped out like he had just won a big award. *Here we go,* I thought smiling down at the pup. *Pretty soon they'll all be escaping the box!*

Chapter 11

Lauren arrived in the beginning of May. She was very excited to be back in her own hometown and with us and immediately made herself at home. Someone donated a bed for her and Chuck and I cleaned out the spare bedroom and had her bed all set up for her. Lauren spent a few days with Flower barking at her. Finally Flower was comfortable with her and then Lauren started handling the puppies (minus Blossom). She was in heaven!

Over the course of the four months Lauren lived with me I learned so much about learning disabilities. It's very unique to each individual person, Lauren no exception. What I can say for sure is that she is truly one of my most favorite people. I adore her no different than I would a biological daughter. She is an incredibly compassionate, empathic person.

***

"To me both Flower and Blossom prove that good things can become of a terrible situation. Two years ago this month my 16-year-old daughter tried to commit suicide. Thank God my husband found her in time.

It has been a challenging two years, but things are

looking better for her. We take one day at a time. Getting through one day sometimes is hard, but we keep our mindset to today, not yesterday as we can't change it, not tomorrow because were never guaranteed tomorrow.

I fell upon this site right after Flower came into your care. How? I do not know. It just popped onto my feed one night. I can say I never miss a live. It has helped me so much.

I suffer from depression and having you guys to look forward to every day is wonderful! I so appreciate you all and what you give to all these special animals. You are all angels and I pray our Lord always blesses each of you!! Thank you."
— Maryanne E.

***

If I had a dollar for every time someone asked me if Blossom was going to "get her wheels" I would be able to buy something quite luxurious. From literally the day we found out she had no front legs well-meaning people on Facebook (and when they met her in person) asked me when she would be fitted for wheels.

I received about six videos of the same six dogs at least a hundred times who all had no front legs and were fitted for wheels. I received dozens of e-mails asking me the same question. I should have just written down and saved the answer and copied and pasted it rather than each time writing out the answer, "Blossom is too young for wheels. We first need to make sure she's healthy," or some version of that. The incessant obsession with Blossom getting "wheels" was trying my patience. It was very time consuming answering each person each time and a great exercise in patience for me.

As of this writing Blossom is about six months old and not fully grown. So as of this moment she doesn't have wheels. We intend to try them with her when the time is right, so I encourage you to follow us on Facebook to see what happens in the future. It's hard to know with her personality whether she will like them or not. She's a very strong-willed little pup. But we will give it a go.

***

The pups were four weeks old and were roly-poly puppies full of adorable, playful energy. One or more were constantly scaling the whelping box. They were playing slow motion with each other a lot. Being rat terrier and Chihuahua mixes, they were something else to watch. They certainly had the alertness and persistence of the breed types. So to manage their increasing energy, size and the fact that there were seven pups we built an outdoor pen area for them to romp and play in daily.

Meanwhile we were receiving little gifts in the

mail and packages left on our doorstep. We received mugs, desserts, fruit, inspirational signs, tea, coffee and notes. People sent messages on Facebook and letters in the mail sharing with us how watching Flower and her buds was impacting their lives. I constantly felt like I had been transported to an alternate reality — almost 20 years running Animal Education and Rescue, largely feeling quite isolated and unrecognized, to now having global attention. I was deeply humbled by the attention and showering of love. While it'll NEVER lead me to having a big head it filled my heart with a deep connection to humans everywhere.

***

"I recently I had bilateral knee replacements. I can't explain how horrific the pain was. They were done at the same time. I literally didn't have a leg to stand on. It was April of 2022 I came across your page of Flower getting ready to give birth.

Once Flower gave birth to her beautiful little buds, I was so involved that it distracted me from my pain at times. Also, your voice was soothing when you would speak to Flower, especially when she was removing Blossom and another puppy from the pool. You are an amazing mom to Blossom. I am absolutely in LOVE with little Blossom as well as Flower. I watch you every night with all the beautiful animals.

You, Chuck, Lauren and Danny are a spectacular, loving, caring family. I can't thank you enough, for Flower, Blossom and Buds, for getting me where I am today. I am still nowhere near a hundred percent but on my way. When I am down I always go to the prior live and re-watch it. I also check throughout the day to see if you're doing an impromptu live.

Please stay as wonderful as you are, and once again many thanks to you, Flower, Blossom and all the other animals for making a better life for me.
Love you always,"
— Theresa
Long Island, Port Jefferson Station
New York

"I lost my 17-year-old Jack Russell, Lucy, in December 2020… She had a dachshund sister, Molly. She was 13 when I lost her in January of this year. Last August, Molly was diagnosed with IVB and was unable to walk for 8 weeks.

3 months later, Molly was diagnosed with a very aggressive mouth cancer and was not a candidate for chemo and radiation. I didn't want to see her suffer and watch her deteriorate, so we made the right decision and gave her the ultimate gift of love by letting her go.

Devastated and heartbroken, I lost both of my babies in a year's time with major health issues. Flower's page kept showing up on my Facebook and I peered into it. Flower having been through what she went through at that horrid place in Alabama had me at the first time I saw her. She is beautiful and so smart.

Blossom, Miss Sassy Pants, never gave up. She is and will always be a little spitfire. Their journeys got me thru one of the most difficult times in my life after losing my babies.

In so many ways, their stories have brought people together from their love around the world. Thru them, my faith in humanity has been restored. Thru them, my broken heart is healing and I don't cry as much for Lucy and Molly and I am learning to adjust to the "new normal".

I thank you, Sandy, for helping me thru your page and for everything you are doing for all of those babies."
— Jennifer C.

***

Morning and evening livestreams were becoming a bigger chore. Weather permitting we did them outside. We had to set up the puppies' play area each time and two at a time bring the pups outside. Then we grabbed a bouncy Flower and had her out there as well. I set up the tripod and started my lives with my usual intro and then let people watch the puppies play, wrestle, tumble and yip. Lauren was a huge help in that way and she was often the one seen on camera since I was the one behind the camera. Lauren is a very quiet person and so that left me doing most of the talking except the times Lauren joined me in a duet of song or I asked her specific questions. We made a good team. Sometimes Chuck joined us, but mostly it was Lauren and me.

***

"I started watching while Flower was pregnant. I thought wow she's huge. She reminded me of my precious baby kisses who passed in 2020. I anxiously waited and watched all throughout those days and nights with such anticipation of the buds' arrival. And then finally she was in labor.

I loved watching her be such a good little mama. I cried and prayed for sweet Blossom. I cried and thanked God many times when Blossom started growing and getting healthier. The love and joy she, Flower, and the other buds brought into this world has been tremendous. I love watching Blossom's adventures. I love watching how she and Flower play.

They and your team make me smile daily. It's such a

> wonderful way to change the world with cuddly love
> and kindness."
> — Maria D.

***

The next phase, as it always is with litters of puppies, was the most labor intensive for us. Flower stopped cleaning up after the pups and so we were left to clean the "poop and pee storm," as I liked to call it. Leave those pups for six hours overnight and you were welcomed with an overwhelming, nauseating smell and disheveled, torn and flung pee pads. Poop and pee was on pee pads, the floor and up the whelping box walls. And since they were active puppies they tracked it all over the place.

The garbage cans outside were overflowing with bags of used pee pads and puppy stuff and we scrambled to find places where we could dump bags since we only had two cans. Until you're in the thick of raising puppies it's impossible to really know all the challenges that one faces. Excess garbage is always a concern for us.

The possibility that Blossom had hydrocephalus still loomed darkly at the back of my mind. I consciously emotionally separated myself a bit from any expectations of outcomes one way or the other. That practice of detaching myself a bit has served me well not to completely fall apart in the past. If she truly had hydrocephalus her prognosis was grim. But

I was also trying to remain optimistic. I knew there was a huge value to the love she was receiving from me, the volunteers and from people all over the globe. Love has incredible healing powers.

So as I waited for her doctor's appointment I tended to her daily needs and ferociously protected her physically. Nikki and I were the only ones that I allowed to hold her since even though she was less than a pound she was a little ball of muscle, energy and determination. With that personality if she wiggled out of someone's grasp, without front legs to break her fall, she could fall to her death.

I'll never forget the milestones Blossom crossed. When she was about three weeks of age she started showing interest in tiny stuffed toys that she was given from followers all over the globe. Then a few weeks later she put a toy in her mouth and gave the toy an impressive robust shake along with a growl. I laughed out loud. She was a spitfire.

When we started giving "mush" to the puppies, a mix of puppy milk and puppy food blended to a soup, she lapped the food up with gusto. The first time I tried to take a toy that she found extra special out of her mouth that pint-sized, 12-ouncer growled impressively at me. That little pup had the determination and gumption of a lion. Her deep, dark brown eyes were bright, inquisitive and sparkled.

When she finally weighed a pound we had a pound party live on Facebook. All the volunteers came to celebrate. Sherri, one of our puppy playmates, brought enough sweets for 10 times the number of people.

***

"I could write a book on what you, your family and others at AEAR have done for my life since April when I came across your page. I was in a deep depression at the time and just trying to pull myself out of that gloomy state. There's no better way to forget about your woes than to help others or focus on good things in life.

I remember you, Sandy, caring so much for Flower and how you helped her to feel better that she was so big carrying her babies and only a little dog. Flower looked up to you with those loving eyes and knew you wouldn't let her down.

I watched at the edge of my seat checking your posts to see if she had her babies and finally the pups finally were born. Every day I would run to watch the videos and share them whenever I could. I have a friend in Germany and hoped the broadcasts would be shared overseas.

Every day was a new adventure. I would talk about what was going on to my family and it cheered me up. Everyone would probably agree this world really needed a pick-me-up after Covid and still searching for the light.

Sandy — you, Chuck, Lauren, Danny, Nikki, AEAR family I feel are part of my family. I enjoy the art nights and love your paintings.

Thank you for inviting us into your home and consistently doing the videos. You were there for me when I needed someone most and there for all those beautiful animals needing a home with love."
— Cathy R.

***

Blossom was very fussy inside her carrier on the way to the animal hospital. She didn't like being confined, so as I drove I had my hand inside the little carrier and on her to soothe her. Peeking over at her she looked up at me with those adorable nearly black eyes. *How could a dog with eyes so dark not look menacing but instead melt my heart,* I often marveled. *It will be what it will be,* I said to myself yet again as I thought of Blossom and her questionable health.

Unfortunately Blossom's animal hospital still wasn't allowing owners to enter without masks on, so I waited in the car as the staff member came and got Blossom. I cautioned that whomever held her must hold firmly so she doesn't wiggle out of their arms. Blossom was a celebrity of sorts there, but I wasn't taking any chances. She carried Blossom inside, in her carrier, like she was carrying a stack of fragile china dishes.

Waiting in the car one second seemed a minute as I waited for the call from the doctor. My phone rang. "Hello."

"This is Dr. Hanover," the veterinarian began. "I have Blossom here. It looks like she's gained weight. I feel pretty confident at this point she doesn't have hydrocephalus. Her skull appears to be almost closed and if it stays open a little bit for her life span it isn't a big deal. That happens sometimes."

Relief washed over me as I thanked him, ended the call and waited for her to be delivered back to me. On the ride home I did a live on Facebook. As I shared the good news tears streamed down my face. I hadn't realized until that time how I had been holding my breath, wishing for the best. A huge burden was lifted. Our girl made it past a deadly health scare. Now we just needed to take the steps necessary to give her an amazing quality of life.

***

"I almost died of septic shock. I was on a ventilator for 2 weeks, in the hospital for 42 days, rehab for 2 weeks. The recovery was hard and long. Watching Flower, her buds and Blossom was the highlight of my day.

Blossom pushed me to recover and not feel sorry for myself. They said it would 18 months to two years.

I'm proud to say that it's 11 months and I'm back to work. I believe in my heart it's all because of the love and power of positive thinking Sandy teaches us. Little Blossom has taught us all so much."
— Tracy D.

Chapter 12

Danya was meditating and projected her intuitive eye toward Earth. She zoomed in her third eye closer and closer yet to a tan-colored house with brown trim. She had marked this as a place where a Lightworker lived. She had been following this soul's journey as it was unfolding.

She watched as the Lightworker, a woman, and her helpers were inside a room of the dwelling with numerous dogs all around them. The woman, her Earth name Sandy, was speaking to an object that Danya knew as a device that allowed the projection of her voice and images that reflected from her object to reach humans all over the world. She listened in.

Sandy was saying, "It's important that we all understand that we have nothing to fear. Look how Flower and her buds are, especially Blossom. Dogs are great teachers. They move through hard times and rise above it. Blossom is a fighter; Flower survived and is thriving. You can too. Love is the answer and being courageous is vital, especially now."

Filled with great joy and hope Danya gently faded from Earth's energy system. She was pleased to be able to share that their help with the burst of light-love that they showered down on Earth had been received and at least one Lightworker was showing humans the way to the greater evolution of their souls. She was confident that other humans were also spreading the word of love and connection all over the world. There is great hope for humanity on Earth, she said to herself.

As it always was and will be wise souls in Spirit will continue to watch over Earth and send tools for humans to utilize. "As It Will Be," Danya glowed her energy high and bright in gratitude.

***

"What have Flower & her buds meant to me? PURE JOY is what comes to my mind. It has been a wonderful journey to see Flower giving birth and raising her babies. Even more wonderful is seeing Blossom thrive because of all the LOVE she has been given. She is truly a miracle and a blessing.

I truly feel blessed meeting you, Chuck and Blossom when I attended the fundraiser and our time at breakfast. Getting to go into Blossom's pen (at the fundraiser) and play with her filled my heart with so much JOY and LOVE.

PURE LOVE also describes the journey with Flower and her buds."
— Barb W.
Commerce Twp., Michigan, USA

The puppies' personalities were starting to come out stronger and I lined up a few volunteers to help with the pups once a day so that I could get a break.

Theresa, Sherri, Ricki and Julie all came a few times a week consistently. For a week or so a young woman named Julia, her mom a long-time volunteer, came by and sat with the pups. But each volunteer that came to help with the pups had to get past the stranger-danger stage where Flower barked and barked at them. After a few times coming over and just ignoring her Flower got to know them and ultimately she'd end up loving their company. The physical clean-up was enormous, but with that came the reward of watching the puppies' antics and silliness that brought us smiles and laughs every single day.

"I started watching Flower when she was pregnant — it just popped up one day. I was smack-dab in the middle of chemo treatments for breast cancer. Most days the most I could do was look at my iPad.

I watched Flower happily bounce around with that big belly every time you posted. Then she had all those sweet babies and one little Blossom had only two legs. Blossom was such an inspiration to me to not give up on those dark days. She wiggled & tried, tried, tried. She kept gaining weight & learning how to get around. I watched her every day & always felt inspired.

I'm finished with chemo now and feel somewhat normal. Blossom is bouncing around parks almost

walking at this point! There's that inspiration again.
I'm going for a walk too.
Love,"
— Cherry B.

The puppies were six weeks old and they reached a new milestone. It was time for them to get their first vaccines and to take good quality photos for our web site so that they could officially be listed available for adoption. That would allow us two weeks to hopefully screen and approve homes for all of them except Blossom. Blossom wasn't ready yet and wouldn't be for a while.

Meanwhile Flower was spending less and less time tending to the puppies. She avoided them getting under her belly to nurse by darting past them or around them. She was like one of those red bouncy balls we used in school, bouncing all over the place. We were gifted a few one-piece outfits we put on her when we could snatch the ever-active little dog and wrangle it on her. It made us laugh every time she wore it because first, she looked adorable, and second, the puppies were always trying to root around the onesie to reach the milkbar. While she wasn't a fan of the outfit she quickly realized it saved her from being nursed on by big and sharp-toothed pups, so she tolerated it being on.

When we took the puppies outside Flower mostly stayed out of the pen where the puppies were romping and playing and instead ran, jumped and bounced around the fenced-in play yard, happy as a lark. She would bark alerts when she heard noise outside the property and checked in on us and her pups periodically as we tended to and watched the pups like mother hens. Flower was an independent dog that was loyal and joyful. Everyone loved her on Facebook. They saw the best sides of Flower and never the dog that was also very fearful of strangers. We never had strangers there when we were filming livestreams because if we did Flower would have only barked non-stop.

Blossom continued to take the most amount of time and required the most attention. When we took Flower and her buds outside I put up a separate play area for Blossom that allowed her to be with her littermates but safely between wire fencing. Because of Blossom's small size and her disability I felt it was necessary before adopting her out to have her see a chiropractor and also research getting her wheels that she could use on occasion, if she could acclimate to them.

Further, in reality, finding a home for Blossom at the same time as her littermates, with so many steps that needed to still be taken, was unrealistic. I wanted her to have the best possible start for a great life, so I wanted to set her up for that before she got adopted...if we could find an appropriate home for her.

***

Summer was upon us and I was relishing in the warmth of the sun and long walks when time allowed it. We continued to rescue other animals and find homes for some. But intake of animals was far greater than adoptions and that was a constant concern. Shelters and rescues everywhere were full and adoptions still remained few and far between. The choices our governments continued to make created a constant trickle-down effect for everyone including us in the animal welfare world.

Getting the e-mails weekly from the transport organization my heart sank every time knowing that I really couldn't take any more animals. The only times I was taking new animals was when it was a dire situation and I was contacted directly. The last animals we took from transport were from a personal text I received from the transport coordinator. They were the last of the dogs still looking for rescue from the Alabama house where Flower came from. So we took a few more. They were three female dogs that were wrecks. They were shut down emotionally, had skin conditions and one had a bottom jaw that was deformed. But we welcomed them in. The one with the deformed jaw has since been adopted while the other two, as of this writing many months later, still wait for forever homes.

As far as the puppies' adoptions, we were getting very few applications for them even though they had received such worldwide attention and the applications we did receive were from outside our area. Typically we prefer to adopt out our animals locally because logistically it's easier, but without many good local applications we considered applications that were farther away.

A local family applied for Flower and I was thrilled. Their application was screened and approved and I set up a time for the family to meet her. It was a single mom and her older kids. The adoption screener told me that she worked from home and that her kids would not be very involved with Flower but that the woman had gotten to know Flower from watching the livestreams and was in love with her. It seemed like a perfect fit. So we scheduled a time for her to meet Flower.

Every day was in full swing the moment Chuck and I opened our eyes. Lauren, while not natural a morning person, made an effort to get up shortly after us. Her job was to tend to the cats while Chuck and I divided chores with the dogs. Typically in the mornings I took care of the puppies. I got used to the explosion of poop and pee that greeted me in the mornings along with stinky, wiggly, happy puppy squeaks and yips. The adorable puppies made up for the dirty clean-up and I often sang to them and talked to them as I cleaned. Livestreams continued twice a day religiously and people continued to tune in and love being part of our lives.

By now I had shared dozens of stories with our Facebook audience. I told stories of my childhood, animals past and present and the goings on of the days. Each story was peppered with moral lessons and messages of strength. I took every opportunity during the lives, as they played out, to share observations that unfolded as opportunities for us to learn and grow.

Having Lauren living with us was a new experience for Chuck and me. Even though I have known Lauren since she was a young child it was the first time she had actually lived with us. Because of her intellectual disabilities, as well as ADHD and emotional challenges, we were continually having to double check any task we gave her to do and monitor her closely. She tended to be impulsive and have poor follow through. That created a lot of extra work for us, but her kindness toward animals and her dedication to us and AEAR seemed to balance the challenges.

Every night before bedtime Lauren always said, "goodnight, love you." She would spontaneously periodically throw her arms around one of us and say, "Bear hug!" Then she'd squeeze us tight. She seemed to do that to Chuck more often and she'd add, "grumpy dad," even though Chuck wasn't grumpy at all. Sometimes she'd call me mom or old lady, the latter I told her that I didn't like. Sometimes she called Nikki old lady too, which again I corrected her. It was something she thought was funny, which really wasn't too funny, but we let it roll off our shoulders.

When Lauren wasn't with her girlfriend or tending to the cats she was either babysitting the dogs for us or tagging along with us. Babysitting the dogs consisted of sitting in the living room looking at her phone while the dogs stayed with her, one, two or three littles on her lap. We'd be elsewhere getting work done. When I went anywhere outside the home, such as to the grocery store, to a thrift store or for a walk, Lauren tagged along. She always wanted to be with me or with us if Chuck and I were together.

My experience raising children hadn't been good in any way, in all honesty. My kids were challenging and to this day we aren't close. Danny, my 14-year-old grandson by birth but son in my heart and all practicality, is a teenager and wants as little to do with us as possible these days.

As a young child my biggest dream was to raise a family and have a home with a fenced yard and a lot of animals. That dream came true, yet my experience of being a mom, despite all my efforts, seemed to cause me more pain than not. I never expected to have had such experiences and so when Lauren came along and wanted to be with us, expressed love to us, she filled a painful wound for me like a healing salve.

After the first month of living with us Lauren said she wanted to live with us permanently and not go back to live with her mom in Maine. Once again we were going round and round about her mom talking to us, but we were beginning to understand just by her living with us temporarily the commitment it would be having Lauren live with us full time. But there were still a lot of unknowns. We had one conversation with her mom, but we knew that we needed regular communication with her to really make sure we were doing the best for Lauren and us.

Chapter 13

The woman who was approved to adopt Flower came over with her son to meet Flower one sunny summer morning. Flower relentlessly barked at her the whole time. The woman was very understanding about it (I had warned her) and really wanted to make it work. But during our time together I found out that her other son was on the autism spectrum and didn't like dogs or loud noises. I also found out that the woman worked outside the home and that Flower would be left alone all day in a crate. I told her that Flower was not a good fit for her and that Flower needed someone who worked from home or was not working. They left and I was relieved that I had been there to learn more about the family. The last thing I wanted…especially for a dog that's been through so much…was for her to end up in the wrong home.

The first two puppies to get approved homes were Lotus and Sprout. Both pups were white with brown markings like their mom and they had the brightest blue eyes, clearly a trait of their unknown father. The couple was from St. Louis, Missouri, and had been following us on our Facebook page since the very beginning. The puppies were soon to be eight weeks old and had their vaccines, microchips and been de-wormed. All the puppies were ready for the next stage of their lives…adoption!

We arranged the adoption of Lotus and Sprout and the family traveled to meet them and take them home. Julie was here at that time, as well as Nikki and of course Lauren and me. It was a joyous occasion for us and marked the beginning of the end of the story of the litter of puppies that spread love and joy all over the world.

The couple arrived with their young adult daughter. They stood near the outdoor pen area, their excitement palpable. Leslie, the mom, was fighting back tears. At the time I was a bit surprised by how emotional she was; it seemed like there was something more to it than just being excited to adopt. As they held their new puppies I snapped some photos of the new family. Julie came down the deck stairs toward them and the waterworks started. Julie is an emotional person and crying during adoptions *is* typical. Well all it took was Leslie seeing Julie crying and walking toward them for Leslie to begin openly crying tears of joy.

For me I was happy for them but more than ready to let them go. I shouldered the brunt of the work with Flower and her puppies. But I also was well aware that the feelings in the air and through cyberland were different this time. People all over the world, from everywhere in the US, South Africa, the UK, New Zealand and more, were deeply attached to Flower and her buds and were mourning their loss of the puppies.

With that in mind I asked Sprout and Lotus's family if they would be okay if I did a live on

Facebook because people all over were having a hard time with the puppies getting adopted. They were good sports and agreed, so I did a short live with the pups being held by their new family. Through tears Leslie shared with the audience that the puppies mean more to her than she can express in words. I knew there must be more to the story than she was sharing then. Later, she shared the whole story on a Facebook group I created for all Flower's puppies' families.

"I'm sharing the story of how I came to adopt Bella (Lotus) and Sprout.

The beginning of this year I had surgery. I had a lot of pain and depression. My soul dog Katy helped me so much in my recovery. She knew when I was not feeling well. When I was in pain and could not sleep, she would cuddle close, sleep next to me, give me kisses and sit by my side.

Katy was so special and smart. She and her brother Jack were rescues. Jack was born deaf...Katy would wake him up and let him know when it was time to eat and go for a walk. She also learned sign language right along with Jack. Katy and Jack were bonded.

My sweet girl was ill and went to heaven on Easter Sunday, April 17th. I know she did not want to leave until I was feeling stronger. Again, I had gone into a depression. A few days after her passing I came across Flower on Facebook. She so reminded me of Katy and acts just like her.

Watching Flower, Sandy, Lauren and the buds just made me feel better. I just know that Katy, my angel, led me to AEAR. I had never heard of or gotten feed from AEAR before.

My husband and I put in an application for Flower. Then I heard she had an approved adopter (that later fell thru) so I put in an application for Lotus and Sprout.

Our journey was meant to adopt these two puppies. They have brought us such great joy. I'm not going to lie...it's been a lot of work.

I was sitting holding Bella and I said, "Give me a kiss." She licked my cheek just like my angel Katy."
— Leslie
St. Louis, MO

***

Kris, the adoption screener for the puppies, was working overtime reviewing and approving adopters. I scheduled appointments with the adopters to meet and take home their puppies. One by one wonderful families came from all over the Midwest to adopt their puppies. Finally the only pups that were left were Basil, one of the brown pups with one blue eye and one brown eye, and Blossom. We hadn't received any other applications for Flower. There were no applications for Basil, but I knew the right family would come along.

Meanwhile I continued to do daily livestreams, reassuring our followers that the puppies were in good hands now and that life is ever-changing and it's best if we can learn to accept that. Every livestream I took opportunities to share my perspective, educate and inspire people. "The one thing we can count on is that nothing ever stays the same. While that may seem unnerving it can also be a blessing," I shared, as I let my Facebook followers see the dogs playing and I provided the dialogue. "I'll give you an example of what I mean by it being a good thing. Yesterday I had a moment where I felt a bit out of sorts; I could feel a touch of anxiety rise up into my chest, an old feeling that fortunately rarely visits me these days. But when it does I catch it earlier.

"So as I sat for a minute in the elevating anxiety that came on for no apparent reason…the weather? some subconscious trigger? I don't know. But in that moment I reminded myself that it will pass and I won't stay in that place. Just the knowing that it isn't permanent reassured me. So, while sometimes we want things to stay the same, it's in our best interest for them not to.

"Besides," I went on, "if we stayed in a safe place in our lives all the time the countless opportunities for growth wouldn't present themselves."

About a week after all the other puppies were adopted I got a text from Theresa, one of the volunteers that had been helping babysit the puppies on occasion. "I'd like to adopt Basil if it's ok with you."

"Really? You said when you started volunteering that you weren't going to adopt a puppy." I remembered vividly the first time Theresa came over she blurted out from the get-go, "I'm not adopting any of these puppies. But I'll help you." I remember laughing because I knew the only reason she would be saying that out of the blue was to remind herself that she wasn't going to fall in love with any of them and want to take them home…even though in reality she knew herself well and would have a very hard time resisting.

"Let's talk about it more, ok? Call me," I said.

Later that day we spoke by phone and she said that she felt bad that Basil hadn't been adopted and that's why she was going to adopt him. I assured her that he certainly WILL get adopted and it was just a matter of time and she shouldn't adopt for that reason. She said, "No, I want him — I do." So I told her to make sure her husband was 100% on board and reminded her of the hard work puppies are. She said she knew and that she would speak to her husband again.

Theresa previously adopted two dogs from us and they were a great dog family. Until she began volunteering helping with Flower and her buds I never knew Theresa personally. But with her at my house regularly I got to know her well. She's a mother and a grandma. She has a quick wit and makes me laugh with her unique perspective on things. She's down-to-earth and kind.

If she adopted Basil I knew she had her work cut out for her. Basil had a confident, feisty and mischievous personality. Of the litter he was one of the pups always getting himself into trouble. He had a reputation all over the world on Facebook as being the most naughty pup of the bunch.

Theresa contacted me the next day and confirmed that her husband was 100% on board, so we arranged for Basil's adoption the next day. Watching Basil walk away in the arms of his new mom I knew that we were beginning a new chapter and the old was now but an amazing memory. We had a lot of work yet to do for Blossom and we needed to get Flower spayed. I also wondered whether this international recognition on Facebook that brought us to a new level of growth would continue now or if things would settle back to what they were before. I reminded myself that I had to have faith in the journey and to just keep my heart open and my intuition sharp, that everything will happen as it should.

Lauren by that time was very settled into the routine of living in our home. She continued to provide me great joy but also some extra work and worry. People on Facebook continued to be very attached to her. Lauren kept insisting she wanted to live with us and so over time and a lot of discussions and soul searching we told her she could live with us. The people on Facebook were thrilled when I announced it.

The plan she had was to go to Maine and spend some time with her mom and brother and then come back some time later. Not to belabor anything, as I write this in October, a month or so since Lauren left, she has decided to stay in Maine permanently. This book is not about Lauren, but I will share with you that I learned so much from Lauren after her spending four months with us. I learned more about myself and about Lauren and the complexities of having someone live with us with developmental disabilities.

I'll miss her, but I trust the universe has my back and this must be the path I am supposed to take, without Lauren as a part of our family or daily life. It was a relief to finally put the issue of when Lauren was coming back to rest. I felt like I was living in limbo to an extent and I was constantly asked by people on Facebook when she was coming back. We could all have closure and move on. I wish her always the very best in her life.

***

With all the puppies gone except Blossom, Flower was spayed and over a period of a week I integrated her with my crew of dogs on the other side of the house. She acclimated seamlessly. She is a party girl by nature and the chaos of my house and the many different dogs suited her just perfectly and they accepted her too.

As far as Blossom was concerned I made a pen area for her in our living room and over a period of time I slowly had her spending more time on our side of the house safe behind her little condo space. Just like her mom she relished in the commotion and had a natural knack for properly building positive relationships with other dogs.

Nikki built a website boutique selling images of Blossom, Flower and more on t-shirts, sweatshirts, mugs and more. Facebook followers were thrilled with purchasing the items and often messaged us after they received their purchases with enthusiastic positive reviews. It was wonderful and a win-win for everyone.

***

Juli, one of my friends and a volunteer, gifted me a bigger stroller for Blossom. The one I dug out of the garage was getting small for her, so the new bright orange one was like the Cadillac of strollers for dogs. I was regularly taking Blossom for walks in her stroller to the park where I let her "run-run-run" and "hop-hop-hop," as I liked to say on social media.

This particular day I chose the park in downtown Libertyville. On our way back I was pushing her along in her stroller, Blossom alert and watching out of her little front window at the scene rolling past, and I thought about Blossom's future. We had researched "wheels" and she wasn't quite old enough for them at almost five months old. I had rearranged my life and my home to accommodate her challenges. I thought about the idea of finding a home for her. I knew it was a long shot to find a perfect home for a dog with ongoing special needs. Then I thought about all the people all over the world who loved her.

Then a vision came before my eyes. I saw Blossom at my home and a vision of the beautiful Earth in its rich blues and greens, as if I was watching Earth from the vantage point of the darkness of space. I saw in my mind's eye the energy of Blossom sending invisible light all over Earth. Then I saw thousands of little dots of light of each person she touched with her love and, really, the collective love of all of us at Animal Education and Rescue to everyone around the world.

In the vision, I saw these lights, twinkling and growing. The lights that represented love spread the love toward, around and within people in communities. It was because of Flower and her buds, especially Blossom, that all that bright and positive change was happening. Then I imagined that I found Blossom the perfect home and saw myself handing her off to whoever that was I chose. Then the vision of Earth that I had seen lit up by love, one by one, turned off their lights like seeing a home's windows lit up at night, one by one, shut off, the rooms dark.

Pushing Blossom along in her stroller, I saw in my mind that Earth became dark. I could hear a deep collective sigh of all those people that were touched by Flower and her buds. They sighed once more and went back to sleep. It was like they no longer were lit up with strength and love. It was in that moment I knew that I could not give Blossom up. Blossom would stay with us forever. We'd make it work. Blossom loved us; we loved her. Besides, we had a bigger mission…to keep spreading love, joy and inspiration around the world and Blossom was leading the way.

***

As of this writing I haven't announced that we are keeping Blossom. Deciding that has been a relief for us that we can plan her future, and Chuck and I have equally bonded to the sassy, high-energy, stubborn, intense, adorable and clever puppy. She's a determined little bugger with a will to live from the moment she entered this life and messages to share with the world. She's a profound inspiration to many, many people and will be the perfect ambassador for love and resilience.

As far as Flower, that's a tough one. We are so torn as far as adopting her out at this point…not that people are applying anyway. It all began with Flower, this whole love fest, this whole awesome, amazing journey we all are riding. She's so happy with us and content.

Realistically she's so hard to place in a home

anyway. She's not good with strangers, not housebroken, barks a lot outside and isn't extremely affectionate or cuddly (more independent). She's also started a new obnoxious habit of biting at the back of our legs and butts when she's excited, and that hurts!

I've done this business a very long time and been a dog trainer for even longer. A big mistake people so often make is thinking that they can fix every behavior issue or personality quirk a dog has. That would be like fixing me so that I wasn't scatterbrained or making me better at math. It'd be like adopting a border collie and expecting them to be a couch potato or adopting a Chihuahua and expecting them to be a seeing-eye dog. You can change some things about an animal, but many things, you need to understand, are who they are.

While I am sure we can teach Flower how to go on walks on leash (which she doesn't currently do) I highly doubt she'll ever be like that super outgoing and stranger-friendly Labrador or Golden retriever. PLUS, she's so HAPPY here and fits like a well-tailored suit. But we certainly weren't looking to commit long term to another dog. We weren't looking to adopt. So we'll see.

Chapter 14

There never is a day that goes by or sometimes even a few hours that doesn't provide me opportunities to learn and grow. I believe that this life I am living is filled with endless opportunities for growth. I am a soul living a human experience working on milestones to a higher truth and understanding of my life and my purpose.

Every year since I started Animal Education and Rescue has provided me countless experiences that were struggles, hardships, victories, suffering, meaningful connections and profound lessons. It has always been that each year is dubbed "The Year of…" It could be the year of the sick cats, or the dog that nearly starved, or the sick husky or the near downfall of AEAR. Since I wrote *The Animal Warrior* I wrote two other books that marked important experiences.

You Are My Sunshine tells the story of my beloved dog Bear, an AEAR volunteer and a senior dog I fostered when she came into our care at age 10 and who I officially adopted at 11. She was the best canine volunteer we ever had and my soul dog. I don't suspect I'll ever feel such a deep connection with any other dog.

A Dog Named Walter is the story of a dog that we had in our care who the night he was adopted escaped his home and ran off into a 200-acre forest preserve. It was the coldest winter and the words *polar vortex* were on the tongues of everyone here in Northern Illinois. I was in the forest preserve each day for weeks trying to catch that dog. It was the winter of Walter and the polar vortex.

The year 2022 is the year of Flower and her Buds and the year that with their help I was able to help spread love and messages of courage, strength and kindness around the world. It was the year that I ended up adopting a sprightly, two-legged dog and when I was able to finally get additional help by hiring someone full time, opening me up to be able to accomplish new and important things in my life's mission. An extra huge blessing was Nikki, one of the bravest, kindest people I know and whose amazing evolution of her soul I was honored to be part of.

Chuck, Nikki, Julie, Lauren and other volunteers shared an amazing, awesome experience that we will never forget and left all of us with a lasting impact. My hope for this book is that its words, stories and messages will continue to share messages of courage, inspiration, joy and love all over the world.

We are all on our own individual journeys of growth. While we all have individual free will to do what we want, learn what we choose and live our lives as we do, we also affect one another deeply. We are both individuals and a collection of souls experiencing this lifetime together.

Readers, don't give up on yourself or in life. Life isn't easy, nor is it meant to be. It's clusters of ups and downs and challenges that can teach us to rise above or we can choose to wallow in where we are or to ignore the lessons.

While we are all on our own individual paths of growth we are deeply connected to each other. What you do affects not only you but everyone else you encounter in your daily travels. The energy you put out into the world may be invisible to the naked eye but is deeply impacting to everyone.

We all have a responsibility to first take care of ourselves, nurture ourselves and love ourselves. This is not selfish but rather is necessary in order to help others actively or passively. We must get beyond fear. The fear that has gripped this world because of the situation and actions of this time in history may on face value appear horrific. It is actually a blessing in disguise.

As the individual must experience hardships and struggles to learn and grow, humanity, collectively, must face struggles in order to grow. Humanity is in the midst of a cracking open. It's our time to choose to rise above fear.

Shut off the news channels and the negative messages everywhere that have an agenda to keep you afraid. That dark energy does not serve you. Become acutely aware of subtle negative messages that the dark souls put out there. Walk away and move away from all of that. They are and it is poison.

Instead use the brain that you are using in this life to learn critical thinking. Think about what you see and ask yourself, "Does this really make sense?" Then dig deep and hard for logical answers. We must be extremely sensitive to the messages that we are getting in order to avoid them or shine light on them, thus snuffing out the darkness. Lightworkers are by nature sensitive, which is why they/we lead the way.

Really see around you that there is so much good happening every day. People have come together in so many ways at this time to help others. There is so much to be grateful for. Write down what you are grateful for and say it out loud. Every day.

Learn new things that fill you up. Take up art, creative writing, jewelry making, pottery, music, whatever, to exercise your creative muscle. It's through creativity that we open a door to a deeper intuition and where we talk to spirits and our higher consciousness.

Find people who are on the path and build networks, create villages of like-minded people and gather together in celebration, song, connections and purpose. This will fill up your heart and soul and remind you that you are never really alone. In creating positive, evolving, proactive groups you are strengthening the collective of humanity in a much bigger way.

When we trust the process and we have faith that we are loved and protected we grow stronger, braver and healthier. We share that wisdom with others through our actions and through our positive energy. We become beacons of love that shine all over the world, taking the world and every living soul — human and animal — to a higher level of evolvement. I'm counting on you to be part of the solution. We got this.

***

The Wisest of the Wise gathered in the Great Hall to look upon the screen that reflected back down to the blue-green planet Earth. The high-frequency buzz of their energy was soothing as they gazed their third eyes at Earth.

Their collective consciousness grew closer and closer toward Earth as images began flashing before them. They saw humans that were helping one another. They heard laughter and conversation. They saw the dark energy beginning to submit as the bright energy of the Lightworkers shining their lights brighter and farther around themselves grew.

Danya navigated her clairvoyance to the humble house in the Midwest to check on the little white-and-brown dog and her little two-legged pup. Looking from above she saw the human Lightworkers – a woman named Sandy, another named Nikki, a man named Chuck, a young woman named Lauren – going about their morning tasks. The mother dog Flower's pups, consciously completely unaware of the influence they have had on the amazing path of light and love they created, were hopping and bouncing about in a room and playing with the other dogs living in the dwelling.

Danya's soul's light expanded in great affection as she watched with great gratitude for this small group of souls. Each human was in their own place in the house, doing their own thing.

In that moment of Earth-time the humans momentarily stopped moving, sure that they could feel something familiar. Warm energy of love and connection, deep and familiar, entered their hearts. Sandy broke out in a melody, *"I think I'll go for a walk outside now, the summer sun's calling my name..."* and twirled in a circle. Chuck reached down and pet the gray cat rubbing up against his leg. Danny, in his room, picked up his ferret Rigby, turned him upside down and stroked his belly. Lauren smiled and scooped up a puppy. Nikki lifted Flower up and nuzzled her face in Flower's neck. In that moment and so many more they were connected to all.

***

"I came across a video, where I saw this little dog. She amazed me. She drew me in. She wagged more than I'd ever seen a dog wag and was just the happiest I had ever seen.

Then I noticed, oh my gosh, she's pregnant... How is she so happy and able to move like that with that huge belly? So I started watching religiously, excited to see her and these babies. I fell in love with her.

The babies were coming and I was so excited! Then everyone saw Blossom had no front legs. Although I loved all of them, she became my heart.

I then fell in love with you guys. I felt like you were my family. You made my days so happy and something to look forward to. You've helped me and so many others with our worrying, depression and anxiety. Every day I wait to hear you for the day, with or without babies.

Flower gave us love and you gave us love and a future. You truly are a fairy angel.
With love,"
— Roselyn
Antioch, Illinois

"I began to follow Flower and her buds when Flower just came to you. It meant a lot to me to have the joy to watch her and her buds from the beginning. We lost our Danish/Swedish farm dog in December 2020 and for me it was a blessing to see how it went for Flower and all her buds.

Then I started to follow Blossom, such a cutie. She is lovely and strong and a clever girl who sends out love to many people all around the world.

Thank you for sharing these lovely dogs and other animals you have. It brings me lot of joy and happiness.
Sending you all my best regards from the North of Sweden,"
— Rauni S.

"Flower and her buds have been a blessing. My life has changed because of them and the love that has been spread all over the world. I was very discouraged not knowing what I would do missing my husband and I found Animal Education and Rescue on my Facebook.

I love Flower and Blossom and everybody that's involved with Animal Education and Rescue. Things have changed so much for me and my willingness to keep going instead of wanting to give up."
— Frances P.

"What a journey this has been and I've loved every minute of it. We lost our baby girl, our 10-year-old Jack Russell, Holly, just over a year ago and miss her every single day.

Following Flower, Blossom and the other buds these last few months has been amazing for me and wow it helps so much. I also had to stop doing my job in February as I have health issues and will be having spinal surgery in just under two weeks.

Keep up the good work. I need you. We all need you."
— Denise B.

"Blossom means so much to me. She is inspirational to me. We both have physical limitations. She inspires me to keep going because she is doing so well. I smile when I see her moving and hopping so well.

I had a car wreck two years ago and can still barely walk. I had many injuries, but it is my broken hip that still has me in pain and unable to do things I once did. I walk slowly with pain and a limp. I cannot bend. I cannot even put on my own sock or tie my shoes.

When I feel like giving up I see Blossom's video with her moving so well and I know I have to keep moving as well.

Thank you, Sandy and Blossom."
— Stacy F.

"Flower and her buds couldn't have come at a more perfect time for me. My cute Chihuahua mix that I had rescued when he was a baby was just diagnosed with cancer. I was having such a hard time coping with this.

Flower and her buds brought me so much joy. Philly, my pup, and I would watch all the live videos together and were rooting for her all the way from San

Francisco, CA!

Philly has since passed and I will always remember Flower and her buds as part of his final journey."
— Cassandra T.

"I lost our Bichon Frise in November and not long afterwards I came across Flower when she was about to give birth to her babies.

It really helped me after losing my beautiful girl and I have followed this page ever since. I do believe it stopped me thinking about her so much. I was so focused on Flower and her babies, which I followed every day, and I still am. So thank you so much."
— Gail H.

Flower and Her Little Buds

Hoppin' Blossom

Blossom, Small But Mighty

Blossom and Flower

Flower and Blossom

Flower

Flower and Blossom Romping in the Woods

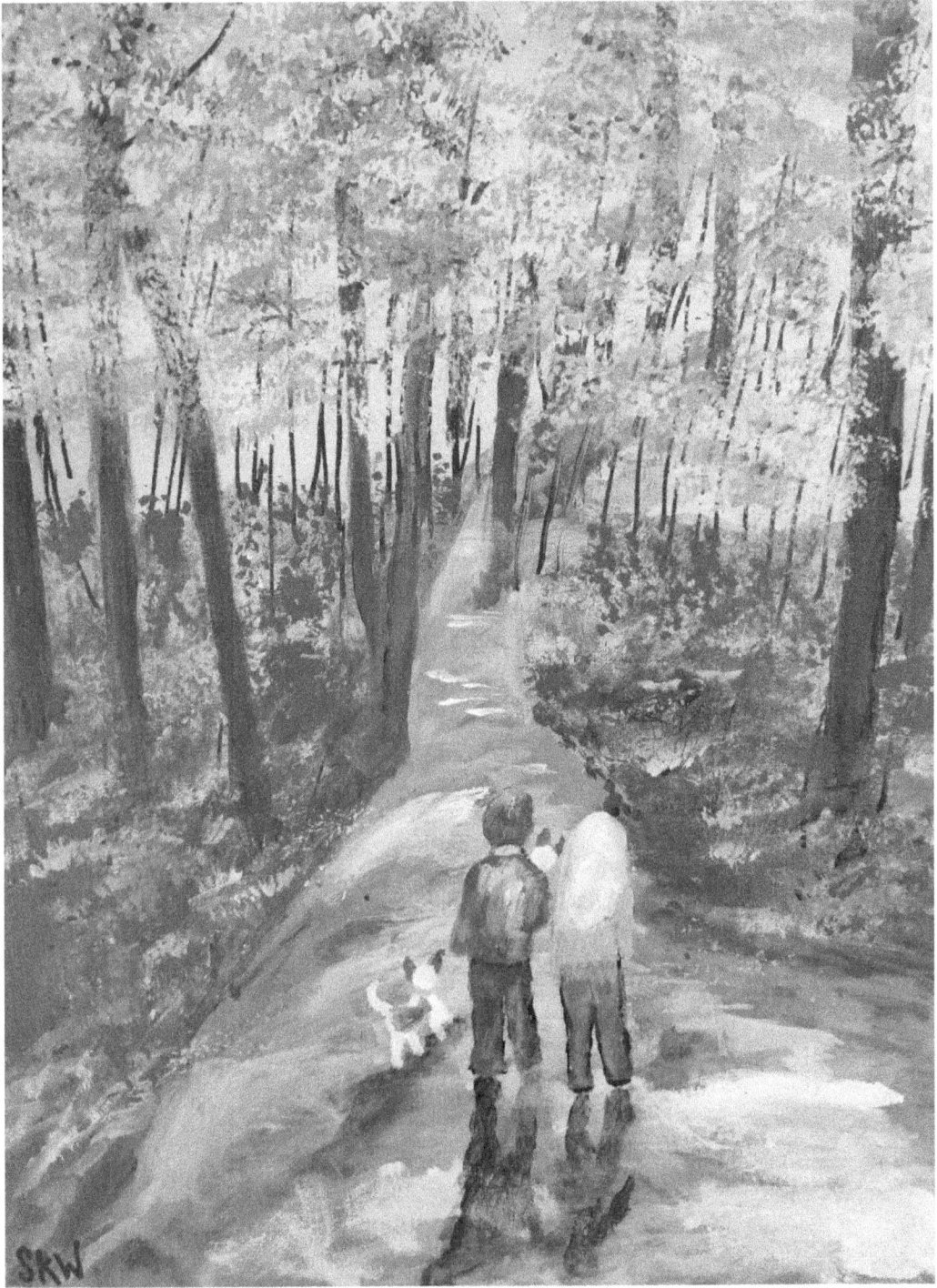

Autumn Stroll in the Forest Preserve
with Blossom and Flower

The AEAR Team
From left: Nikki, Julie, Lauren, Sandy and Chuck
(Photo Credit: Janelle Rominski)

About the Author

Sandy Kamen Wisniewski is the founder and director of Animal Education and Rescue, a charitable rescue and humane society. She is a lifelong writer and published author of dozens of newspaper and magazine articles and six books:
Flower, Her Buds and a Special Little Blossom
A Dog Named Walter
You Are My Sunshine
The Animal Warrior
I Can't Stop Shaking
How to Start Your Own Pet Sitting Service

Sandy is an intuitive healer, artist and inspirational speaker. She strives to come from a place of love to educate and inspire those around her.

Sandy shares her home with her husband Chuck, her son Danny and countless rescue animals — some that come and go and others that stay for life.

www.aear.org
www.mindfulspirit.net
www.sandykamenwisniewski.com

Follow Sandy on Facebook at:
Animal Education and Rescue
Sandy Kamen-Wisniewski

www.ingramcontent.com/pod-product-compliance
Lightning Source LLC
Chambersburg PA
CBHW062044090426

42740CB00016B/3013